John Jeremiah Daniell, Canon Jackson

The History of Chippenham

Compiled from Researches by the Author, and from the Collections of Rev. Canon Jackson

John Jeremiah Daniell, Canon Jackson

The History of Chippenham
Compiled from Researches by the Author, and from the Collections of Rev. Canon Jackson

ISBN/EAN: 9783337203634

Printed in Europe, USA, Canada, Australia, Japan

Cover: Foto ©ninafisch / pixelio.de

More available books at **www.hansebooks.com**

David M Barclay

1914
St Paul's Rectory
Chippenham

THE
HISTORY OF CHIPPENHAM

R. F. HOULSTON
PRINTER, CHIPPENHAM
AND AT BATH

CHIPPENHAM MARKET PLACE, with Old Shambles, Inns, Town Pump, &c.   A.D. 1820.

THE
HISTORY OF CHIPPENHAM

BY THE

REV. J. J. DANIELL

RECTOR OF LANGLEY BURRELL, WILTS

AUTHOR OF

"The History of Warminster," "Life of George Herbert,"
"History of Cornwall," &c.

COMPILED FROM RESEARCHES BY THE AUTHOR, AND

FROM THE COLLECTIONS OF

The Late REV. CANON JACKSON, F.S.A.

RECTOR OF LEIGH DELAMERE, WILTS

CHIPPENHAM AND BATH:
R. F. HOULSTON, PRINTER, BOOKSELLER, AND STATIONER
LONDON: HOULSTON & SONS, PATERNOSTER SQUARE
1894.

PREFACE.

SOME years ago Canon Jackson put into my hands a Portfolio of "Chippenham Papers," with the permission to make of them what use I pleased; I made copious extracts. After his death, these Papers were again entrusted to my care. On a third occasion, at my request, the Society of Antiquaries allowed me to examine them. I thus became well acquainted with their contents. They were not arranged in order, nor with any immediate view to publication, but from the character and number both of manuscript notes and printed papers, it was evident the Canon contemplated dealing at large with the subject. He had had the privilege, on some earlier day, of examining the documents in the Borough Chest, and he made such diligent research among them, and copied and summarised so much serviceable material that he had forestalled to a great degree Mr. F. H. Goldney's valuable "Records of Chippenham." Mr. Goldney's transcripts, however, yet remain to be fully digested, so as to furnish a chapter not yet written in a history of Chippenham.

PREFACE.

I foresaw the probability that, as the "Jackson Papers" had left the County, their very existence would soon be forgotten; I therefore proposed to myself to cull out of the Canon's *Memorabilia*, manuscript and printed, those facts which had reference of immediate interest to Chippenham, and to frame a narrative which I might supplement by my own reading and observation.

The result is this present HISTORY of CHIPPENHAM —and I cannot but believe that the people of Chippenham will be gratified with what we have written.

JOHN J. DANIELL.

RECTORY,
LANGLEY BURRELL.

CONTENTS.

		PAGE
I.	SITE OF CHIPPENHAM	1
II.	MANOR OF CHIPPENHAM	3
	SHELDON	13
	ROWDON	14
	MONKTON	16
	COCKLEBURY AND FOGHAMSHIRE	16
	ALLINGTON	17
III.	CHIPPENHAM FORESTS	19
IV.	GEOLOGY OF CHIPPENHAM	24
V.	RIVER AVON, WELLS, AND SPRINGS	28
	LOCKSWELL SPRING	31
VI.	THE GARDEN OF WILTS	35
VII.	STANLEY ABBEY	48
VIII.	CHIPPENHAM PARISH	55
	THE BOROUGH	56
	THE CHARTERS	58
	THE TOWN HALL	63
	MEMBERS OF PARLIAMENT	67
	THE BAILIFFS	75
	THE TOWN	82
	TRADE	90
	THE BRIDGE	93
	THE CAUSEWAY	95

CONTENTS.

		PAGE
	THE PLAGUE	98
	THE SCHOOL	103
	THE FIRE OF LONDON	105
	RIOTS	107
IX.	THE MANOR OF OGBOURNE St. GEORGE	112
X.	NOMINA VILLARUM	113
XI.	SHERIFFS OF WILTSHIRE	116
XII.	MAUD HEATH'S CAUSEWAY	120
XIII.	CHIPPENHAM DURING THE CIVIL WAR	127
XIV.	PARISH CHURCH OF ST. ANDREW	141
	CHANTRIES IN CHIPPENHAM CHURCH	143
	THE VICAR OF CHIPPENHAM	146
	THE CHURCH LANDS	149
	THE REGISTERS	154
	THE COMMUNION PLATE	159
	THE BELLS	160
	CHURCHWARDENS' RECORDS	160
	CHANTRIES	162
	MONUMENTAL INSCRIPTIONS	165
XV.	WEST TYTHERTON	187
	EXTRACTS FROM A MEMORANDUM BOOK OF THOMAS GARDINER	189
XVI.	ST. PAUL'S CHURCH	193
XVII.	CELTIC AND SAXON WORDS	195
XVIII.	DISTINGUISHED NATIVES OF CHIPPENHAM	209
XIX.	PERSONS OF NOTE WHO HAVE LIVED IN THE NEIGHBOURHOOD OF CHIPPENHAM	217
XX.	ADDENDA	242

HISTORY OF CHIPPENHAM.

I. SITE OF CHIPPENHAM.

LET it be supposed that in the early Saxon days, say about A.D. 700, the King of the West Saxons is on a hunting expedition in one of his fine forests in the north part of his dominions. He is accompanied by a noble cavalcade of Princes, Thanes and Chiefs mounted on gallant steeds, attended by huntsmen, archers, and spearmen, and these followed by hounds of mighty bone or fleetness, according as they would be needed for the chase of wolf or deer.

Say that they have been hunting all the fine autumnal day, and at eventide prepare to form a resting place for the night on the banks of a beautiful stream in the depths of the forest. At sunrise, before their eyes appears a fine grassy knoll, rising from the river-banks high above the surrounding plateau, so elevated, so pleasant, and so sunny, that the royal party exclaim with one voice, that the site is worthy of being the seat of the "King's Lodge" in the Forest.

So said—so done. Soon rises the VILLA REGIA, as the Latin chronicler names it, the hunting seat of the King, though at first a collection of wooden houses, mere log-huts, yet increasing year by year in size, character, and importance, with a growing population of needful attendants, till the neighbouring oaks are felled, and the land is cleared, and *Villans*, and *Cozcets*, and *Serfs* till the Lord's Farm, and cattle, and corn, and articles of various merchandise, and all the rude activities of primitive life gather round the Royal Dwelling; and they build a Church, that God be not forgotten in the wilderness, and they cleave ways through the woods, and the coracles pass up and down the river, and the busy traders barter their commodities, and they call the settlement CEAP-HAM, *the Marketing-place*—in the Forest.

II. MANOR OF CHIPPENHAM.

THERE is no trace that the Romans ever occupied any station in this immediate neighbourhood. Two great Roman roads passed near the site of Chippenham, the Foss Way, on the north, from Bath by Sherston and North Wraxall, and another on the south by Lacock, through Spy Park, past Wans House, to Marlborough; but though there are proofs of Roman habitation at Studley, Bromham, Lacock, and Box, and elsewhere, no Roman remains have been discovered in Chippenham.

The name *Chippenham* is purely Saxon. The root is the Saxon word *Ceap*, meaning any kind of merchandise; thence we have *Ceapinge*, a place where goods are sold, a market-place, as *The Cheaping*, a large green in the town of Wottonunderedge; *Cheap* Street in Bath, *Chipping* Sodbury, *Chipping* Norton, and many others, retaining their Saxon name to this day. Wycliffe, in the first translation of the Bible into English, renders St. Matthew xi. 16, "It is like unto children sitting in the *Chepynge, i.e.* the market." *Ham* is also Saxon for *Place* or *Village*.

Early in Saxon days Chippenham is dignified by becoming a Royal Manor. It is uncertain whether it came into the hands of the Saxon monarch as he was the representative of the FOLC-LAND, or whether he held it as private property by purchase. It is certain that before A.D. 800, Chippenham, with the large Manors of Corsham, Melksham, Calne, Warminster, and other valuable seigniories, formed part of the TERRÆ REGIS, the Crown Lands. The King was by far the largest landholder in Wilts, and, like other freemen, depended for his income on the successful cultivation of his farms. These Manors, or Parishes, as they were afterwards called, included houses, cottages, farms, barns, granaries, and stalls for cattle, and the lord journeyed from one Manor to another as his pleasure or necessities dictated. Some of the Royal Manors enjoyed peculiar immunities and privileges, as Chippenham: but in return, the tenants of this Manor were bound to provide the King, and all his suite, with board and lodgings for one night, whenever his Majesty was pleased to visit his country estate.*

Chippenham, by name, first appears in history in A.D. 853; it was then a VILLA REGIA, a country seat of the Kings of Wessex, and it must have been one of the chief Royal residences, for it is recorded—

---

* This obligation to entertain the King, which was probably exacted of all Royal Manors, was demanded and allowed by Sir James Thynne, Lord of the Manor of Warminster, who received King Charles II at Longleat in 1663, and by Lord Weymouth, who entertained King George III, the Queen and Princesses, on Sep. 13, 1786.

Ethelwulf, King of England, with royal splendour, celebrated the marriage of his daughter Ethelswitha, with Buthred, King of Mercia, in the Villa Regia, the King's Country House, which is called Chippenham.

This Royal seat was not even now much more than a collection of wooden houses, yet it had a Church, probably of stone, (for those early Christians gave their best to God, and we find in Wilton Minster, as early as A.D. 968, "a full fayre chapell of lyme and stone,") and large manorial buildings, though of humble construction. But it would be the most populous and important settlement for many miles around, as it gave name to the Hundred in which it lies. The parishes and places in the Hundred of Chippenham (much then as now), were

Alderton	Kellaways	Luckington
Box	Kingswood	Pewsham
Bremhill	Kington West	Sherston Magna
Castle Combe	Lacock	Sherston Parva
Chippenham	Langley Burrell	Slaughterford
Corsham	Leighdelamere	Sopworth
Ditteridge	Littleton Drew	Wraxhall North
Easton Grey		Yatton Keynell,

with parts of Christian Malford and Hullavington.

By unbroken tradition the actual site of the King's residence in the Manor was that high ground now occupied by the houses above the Angel Hotel, Chippenham. The area in front of them has borne always the name of the PALACE SQUARE. Foundations of very old buildings have been discovered, and a decayed spiral stair case, cut in steps out of a solid trunk of a huge oak (forming originally the ascent to a turret,) was removed from that site about 1820, and left to perish by exposure to weather in a timber yard. In the garden behind the Square is a mound of earth of considerable height, which no doubt at one time bore a watch-tower, from which for ten miles around, might be observed the movements of an invading host. Before the plateau was covered with houses, when the land lay open down to the river on three sides, the scene must have been extremely beautiful. Go stand on the watch-tower—dismiss all the buildings of the town from sight, and imagine a clear, open grassy upland sloping gracefully down to the river-side, but environed on every side by the grand timber trees of the primeval and interminable forest, and you will not wonder why the Saxon King chose that lovely elevation as the site of his royal town.

In A.D. 866, in the reign of Ethelbert, when Alfred, afterwards King, was seventeen years old, a horde of wild invaders, from the north of Europe, under the general name of Danes, landed on the east coast, and pressing west-ward by Reading, fought a battle at Englefield.

"After that," says one of the chroniclers, "they fought at Chippenham; and there was Hubba slain; and a great hepe of stones layed coppid up, where he was buried."

A large barrow in Lanhill mead, about three miles from Chippenham, a long pile of stones, 60 paces in length, was thought by John Aubrey to be Hubba's burial place, but it is much earlier than the ninth century.

Prince Alfred at first defeated the Danes, and retarded their westward advance, but, overwhelmed by numbers, the Saxon troops fell back into Somerset, and though Chippenham was now a considerable town, and the peninsula on which it was built, could, by raising a rampart on the south side of the plateau, be rendered a fairly defensible post, Alfred was obliged to abandon it.

The Anglo-Saxon Chronicle recites,—" This year, 878, during midwinter, the Danish army stole to Chippenham, and sat down there." Asser adds—" *Et ibi hiemavit*—and there wintered." The *Metrical Romance of the History of the Angles* enters into fuller details:

> " Then at Christmas the felon Danes,
> Who had sworn to keep the peace,
> Broke it like knaves,
> And marched into Wessex.
> At Cippenham they halted for a time,
> And took pleasure in doing mischief.
> They destroyed houses and crops,
> Churches and their religious.
> They drove the people from their country,
> And put many in prison."

But next year, Alfred having rallied his forces in Selwood Forest, overthrew the Danes, under Guthrum, in the great battle of Ethandune, and concluded a treaty at Chippenham, by which they agreed to receive the Christian Faith. The Danes withdrew to Cirencester, and the VILLA REGIA of Chippenham once more received its lawful lord.

Alfred died in 901, and was buried at Winchester. He left by his will his Chippenham Manor to his youngest daughter Alfritha, (married to Baldwin, Count of Flanders,) for her life.* In the reign of Edward the Confessor, about 1042, it was again in the King's own hands. Then were the golden days of Chippenham.

* In 940, Edmund, King of the Anglo-Saxons, grants to his servant Wilfric, lands and tenements at Langley, and the deed is confirmed by the King at—*celebri loco*—the wellknown town—of Chippenham.

Under the mild rule of the saintly monarch, the Manor paid no taxes or assessments. Oh, happy Chippenham! Its inhabitants knew nothing of Income and Property Taxes, Poor Rates, Highway Rates, Land or House Tax. Now, in the year 1893, under the iron rule of an Imperial Parliament, a County Council, and a Local Board, the taxes levied on the parishioners of Chippenham amount to an annual assessment of £6312.

But—the Saxon rule is over—Harold lies dead on the field of Hastings—William the Norman is King of England. The conquered land is parcelled out amongst the Norman warriors. Saxon Thanes become labourers on their own soil. The estates which formerly pertained to the Saxon Monarchs, and Chippenham with them, pass by stern consequence, with all their franklins, burghers, villans, and serfs into the tenure of the Norman Sovereigns.

In midwinter, 1085, William projected the Grand Inquest of all England, the Domesday Survey. The great volume still exists as fresh and perfect as when the scribe first put pen to parchment. Chippenham Manor is thus recorded under the division "TERRÆ REGIS."

> "The King holds Chippenham. King Edward held it. It paid no geld, neither was it assessed in hides. The land is 100 carucates. In desmesne are 16 carucates, and 28 serfs. There are 48 villans, and 45 bordars, and 20 cottars, and 23 swine-herds. Between them all they have 66 carucates. There are 12 mills of the value of £6, and 100 acres of meadow. The wood is 4 miles in length and breadth. The pasture is

2 miles long, and 1 mile broad. This manor, with its appendages, provides one night's entertainment for the King with all its customs (or with all his retinue), and is worth £110 by tale. Bishop Osborne holds the Church of this manor, with 2 hides, from the time of King Edward. One of these hides is Thane-land; the other belongs to the Church. The whole is worth 55 shillings. To this manor belongs a certain land which King Edward had given to Ulviet his huntsman, and which was part of his desmesne. This is now in the estate of the King, and it is reckoned for one hide. The land is 2 carucates, and there are 3 serfs and 4 villans, and 4 coscets with one carucate. The pasture is 4 furlongs long and one furlong broad. It is worth £3. In the estate of this manor is half a virgate of land, which was Thane-land. Edric held it in the time of King Edward."

The Hide is ever of uncertain area; it varied from 40 to 150 acres, according to the quality of the land; it was the estate of one large household, sufficient to maintain one family. The Hide included all the land, the Carucate only arable.

The desmesne was the King's Farm, called the In-Land, cultivated by the King's labourers; the Out-Land was let out in small copyholds to Villans, Bordars, Cottars and other tenants, by service of crops, cattle, and work.

Serfs were native Britons, held in bondage by the Saxon conquerors; the serf was the absolute property of his master, a chattel to be bought and sold at pleasure; he had no standing, no protection in law, but by a statute of Canute, he might not be sold to a heathen trader without fault. In the course of years, by the intervention of the clergy, the serf obtained many alleviations of his hard lot; he was allowed to cease from labour from sunset on Saturday to sunset on Sunday, and on High Festivals; by the laws of Ina, if a master compelled a serf to work on Sunday, the offender was fined 30 shillings, equal to £100 of present money. Alfred very much modified the severity of serf labour, and it is a question whether the serf in Alfred's days, and on his manor of Chippenham, was not in a better position as regards his domestic comforts, than the labourer in the parish of Chippenham now. Every serf received two good loaves a day, besides meals at morn and noon: by extra work, he could lay up money enough to purchase his own and his family's freedom; it seems, if he became possessed of five hides of land, he might rise to the rank of a thane, or even of earl.

The Villan was a Tenant Farmer, a responsible man, who quitted the lord's dues more by service than rent; he must ride, carry, and work for his lord, sow and reap, hew the deer fence, watch at war, pay tithe and Church rate.

The Bordars held land by some particular service, but it is not clear what office they performed; they paid no rent in money.

The Cottar must pay his Church dues, and two and two fed one staghound; he had a right to two oxen, one cow, six sheep for stocking his land, and seed for seven acres; tools for his work, and furniture for his house; but when he died everything he was possessed of belonged to his lord.

The Coscets were also small tenants, but of a higher order; they were bound to work all day on Monday for the lord, or three days every week in harvest; they paid no rent, but must discharge Church dues at Martinmas.

On Chippenham Manor were twenty-three Swineherds; they were franklins or freemen, who paid rent in pigs for the privilege of feeding swine in the Forest; they rendered each about fifteen porkers every year, and provided a horse for the In-Land, with other dues. Only eighty seven Swineherds are registered in all Wilts Domesday, and of these, the large number of twenty-three were attached to the important Manor of Chippenham, in close contiguity to great forests.

Mills are carefully recorded throughout the Survey. Twelve in Chippenham lordship are a very large number; being on a good stream, and water power regular and abundant, they were very valuable and paid high rents. Foundations of old mills are to be found on all the water-courses round Chippenham. The Town Mill on the Avon, near Chippenham Bridge, has been incessantly at work, probably for a period of twelve hundred years.

From the number of persons named as living on Chippenham Manor, about 180, and these heads of families, we may make an approximate estimate that the population was 650. Domesday registers in all about

230,000 souls; hence it is calculated the population of England in the middle of the eleventh century was a little over one million persons.

The population of Chippenham parish, during the nine decades of the present century, has ranged as under:—

A.D.				A.D.		
1801	.	3336		1851	.	4999
1811	.	3410		1861	.	5396
1821	.	3506		1871	.	5202
1831	.	4333		1881	.	5191
1841	.	5438		1891	.	*5392

There is no known reference to Chippenham, town or manor, through all the Norman or Plantagenet reigns. Concerning its public history there is an unbroken silence of three hundred years. It is not mentioned in connection with the wars of Stephen and Maud, probably because no strong castle was erected here, and it was never fortified and enclosed by walls. From 1100 to 1300, Malmesbury, Devizes, Trowbridge, all defended by fortresses, frequently appear in the chronicles, which say nothing of weak and unwalled towns, such as Chippenham, Melksham, and Warminster.

Nevertheless, Chippenham, through all those years, had a local history of much interest.

For centuries it had remained an integral portion of the personal desmesne of the Saxon Kings. Early in

* The population for 1891 belongs to the parish as altered under the Divided Parishes Act; detached parts of Chippenham, containing 303 inhabitants, were transferred to other parishes, while a population of 139 was added to Chippenham.

Norman times it ceased its connection with the Crown, and was broken up into the small manors of Sheldon, Rowdon and Lowdon.

SHELDON.

Sheldon Manor, with the lordship of the Hundred of Chippenham, was granted by one of the Norman Kings to William de Beauvilain. This Knight, or his heir, seems to have been in Normandy when that province was invaded by the King of France; and when, by the pusillanimity or apathy of King John, it was torn from the Crown of England, the Manor and Hundred of Chippenham fell, *in escheat*, by the King's prerogative, into John's hands, who conferred them on his son, Prince Henry, afterwards Henry III. In 1211, Henry, by letters patent, conveyed the estate to Sir Walter de Godarville. This family ran out in Joan de Godarville, who was married to Sir Godfrey Gascelyn, and thus he became owner of Sheldon and lord of Chippenham. The Gascelyns held the property 174 years, residing in their mansion at Sheldon; during this time they obtained from the Crown the grant of two Fairs for the town of Chippenham; and probably from this connection with the family, the borough bears their arms—On a golden field, ten blue billets, with a red label. In the reign of Henry VI, the two properties were sold to Walter, Lord Hungerford, for £1000, equal to present money, £10,000.

Sheldon remained in the Hungerford family about 150 years, again and again forfeited, but again and again recovered. In 1684, Sir Edward Hungerford having reached the crisis of extravagance, was compelled to break up his noble inheritance, and Sheldon was sold to Sir Richard Kent, M.P. for Chippenham, whose estates fell into Chancery, and Sheldon passed into the possession of Sir Richard Hart, then to Norris, of Nonsuch House, and now belongs to Sir Gabriel Goldney, Bart.

On Lord Hungerford's attainder in 1540, the liberty or lordship of Chippenham, was then (and has ever since remained) severed from the manor of Sheldon. Edward VI sold the fee simple to Lord Darcy, of whom it was purchased by Sir William Sherrington, of Lacock. In 1650 it belonged to the Danvers, of Dauntesey. It was forfeited on the attainder of Sir John Danvers, the regicide; and James II granted it to Charles Mordaunt, Earl of Peterborough, one of whose descendants sold it to Joseph Neeld, Esq. of Grittleton.

ROWDON.

While this part of the Manor of Chippenham remained in the Crown, Richard I charged it with a pension of £7 10s. 0d. to "*Hodierne the Nurse.*" Henry III in 1250, granted it to Lady Agnes de Roudon; her son sold it to Nicholas Husee, whose family held it till 1392. Their coat bore Three boots sable, which is the second of the shields of the borough of Chippenham. The palm tree, on which the shields depend, and the motto "UNITY AND LOYALTY," were granted by the Heralds' Office. Out of the rent of £7 10s. 0d., the Nurse's pension, which reverted to the Crown, Edward I granted £5 a year to the monastery of Ivy Church, near Salisbury: the lands, which were charged with this payment, then partly a down called "*Ivy Common*, with *the Ivy House and the islands in the Ivy*," bear the name of *Ivy* to this day. In 1434 Rowdon was bought by Lord Hungerford, who, ten years before, had purchased Sheldon.

Through various generations of that family, some of whom built Rowdon House on the banks of the Avon it passed to Sir Edward Hungerford, M.P. for Chippenham, and from him to Edward Hungerford, the Spendthrift, who, as it is said, at a gambling match of bowls, staked his last chance, saying, "HERE GOES ROWDON."

It was mortgaged to Sir Richard Kent, and, in 1698, was bought by an ancestor of the Longs of Rood Ashton. LOWDON, a part of this manor, was granted by the Crown to the family of Pavely; they sold it to the Gascelyns, who also held Sheldon, and who sold both to the Hungerfords. In course of years this property became separated into small freeholds. But the tithing still bears the name Manor.

John Aubrey describes Rowdon House, as "*a large well-built Gothique house, square, and a Court within; about the house a mote; a fair hall very well furnished with armour. Here were a number of scutcheons in the windows.*"

MONKTON.

This royalty, extending into the town of Chippenham, was given by the Empress Maud, (mother of Henry II) to the Priory of Monkton Farley. It thus gained the name of Monkton, *i.e.* "Monk's Town," but it does not appear that there ever was a Religious House on the land. Henry VIII granted it to Sir Edward Seymour; the heiress, Elizabeth Seymour, carried it on her marriage into the family of the Bruces, Earls of Aylesbury, from whom it passed to the families of Esmeade and Edridge. This estate had a right of depasturing in the Forest, and held many wastes there, which in succeeding years were let out on long leases.

COCKLEBURY AND FOGHAMSHIRE.

In Aubrey's time " the inhabitants of Cockleborough said that anciently it was a *borough;* " he means a *tithing.*

" It hath its denomination from the petrified cockles which are in great plenty found in the stones here. Anciently London Road was here." AUBREY.

The old road from Bath to London did not run through the town, as Chippenham Bridge was only wide enough to allow the pack horses a way: but London Road turned down through the narrow winding lane in Foghamshire, up Monkton Hill, through Cocklebury over Langley Common, (where it is still traceable, and bears the name of "London Way", thence through a ford of the Avon, to the present London Road, near Harding's Copse.

Foghamshire, called in the musters of 1539, the "tithing of Vokan or Voghan," was not in the borough of Chippenham; it seems to have formed part of the Manor of Rowdon.

ALLINGTON.

Allington was given by Stephen to the Prioress and Nuns of Martigny, on the Upper Rhone; in the reign of Edward I. they transferred the estate to the Priory of Monkton Farley, near Bath; at the Dissolution, Henry VIII. conveyed it to Sir Edward Seymour, afterwards the Protector Somerset. Algernon, Duke of Somerset, dying without heirs male, was succeeded in some of his estates by Sir Charles Wyndham, and from the Wyndhams, Earls of Egremont, Allington was bought by Mr. Joseph Neeld, in 1844.

In 1623 Sir Gilbert Prynne lived at Allington House; he and his lady are buried in Chippenham Church; the house is now used as a barn, but mantle-pieces and mullioned windows still may be seen, with the arms of Prynne quartering Davys built into a wall.

Fowlswick is a farm on the extreme N. W. corner of Chippenham parish, in the tithing of Allington; Aubrey writes of it:

"Here is an ancient howse with a faire mote about, and with cross barred windowes, then according to the fashion of those times, which were so infested with robbers and house breakers; the retayners here, well fed, and led an idle lazie life, hence those evils."

In 1303 it was part of the estate of John Burel, of Langley, who granted to Elyas Escudemor, lord of Hardenhuish, an acre of land in the East Field of Langley, on the service of a pair of gloves at Easter. In later days Fowlswick belonged to the Jacobs, of Norton, of whom Mr. Neeld bought it.

III. CHIPPENHAM FORESTS.

AUBREY conjectures that the whole island was anciently one great forest, that in Wessex a stag might have ranged from Braden Forest, through Grittenham Forest and Clockwoods, thence to Bowood, Calne and Pewsham Forest, Blackmore and Gillingham Forest, Cranborne Chase, Holt Forest, to the New Forest in Hants.

"Let us imagine, then, what kind of Country this was in the time of the ancient Britons, by the nature of the soil, which is a soure, woodsere land, very natural for the production of oaks especially; one may conclude that this North-Division was a shady, dismal wood; and the inhabitants almost as savage as the beasts, whose skins were their only raiment. The boats on the Avon were baskets of twigs, covered with an ox-skin." AUBREY.

The trees were oak and beech. The elm seems not to have been indigenous to Britain, and yet this noble tree, and its congeners, have taken such root in Wiltshire, and grow so rapidly, that but for the spade and the plough, all the country would, in fifty years, become a dense forest of elms. The Forests around Chippenham were Braden, Bowood, Pewsham and Blackmoor, full of deer, and in all most every barrow, *i. e.* burial mounds raised by the ancient inhabitants, on the downs by the side of the interments are found spear heads of deer's horns, and bones of deer worked into various articles of use and ornament.

Large areas of open ground, unincumbered with timber, were found in every forest, and in course of years these were enclosed for tillage or pasture, and became the sites of villages and towns.

Domesday gives Chippenham Forest as four miles square, but its dimensions must have greatly shrunk by the time of the "Perambulation of Forests" in 1300, when it is described as

"Beginning at the bridge of Stanley, by the highway to the gate of Stanley, through the middle of the town of Stodeley unto the bridge of Samborn, thence ascending the water to the bridge of Fynnam, by the way which leads to the cross before the house of Horne, by the same way to Horseleperde, by the way which cometh from Devizes unto the ash of Lacock, thence to the bridge of Chippenham, as the water of Avon divideth; thence by the water to Merkeden, and thence to the aforesaid bridge of Stanley. The aforesaid metes and bounds enclose the Forest."

Pewsham Forest (within the Forest of Chippenham), extended from the town to Derry Hill: its west side lay toward Lackham. It was fenced round for deer, and might be called the "Home Park."

The Forests remained part of the Crown Lands long after the alienation of other portions of the Manor.

There is a document amongst the records of Chippenham, which describes Pewsham Forest as beginning at "*Fermerie House,*" and ending at "*Hinlond.*" "*Fermerie*" may mean "Infirmary," that is "Hospital" or "Spital," a farm exactly on the southern limit of the Forest, probably a "Convalescent Home" for the Stanley monks. "*Hinlond*" is the large meadow "Inlands," near the town, now called by a strange and meaningless corruption, "Englands."

Another account runs thus:

"Beginning at Lacock Bridge, the Forest Boundary all the way to Chippenham was the river, which continued to define its extent round the north of the town by Monkton Park to the meadow where the river Marden, or Calne water, falls into the Avon. The Marden was then the boundary past Stanley Abbey by Studley to Bowood. A line then ran along Sandy Lane to the road leading to Bowden, and so back to Lacock Bridge."

It was not all forest, as has been said, but it included large tracts of heath land, valuable for pasturing cattle, and many acres of magnificent meadows along the water-courses. The Abbot of Stanley had a right of running all kinds of beasts in Pewsham Forest, and the monks of Bradenstoke, and others, of feeding 50 cows; and all the tenants on the Royal Manor had inherited, from the Saxon Kings, certain valuable privileges of cutting wood, turf, and furze; of feeding cows, pigs, colts, geese, &c.: of digging stone, and even of building huts on the waste, and enclosing what land they pleased for gardens.

James I. granted Chippenham Forest to the Earl of Anglesea, brother of the ill-fated Villiers, Duke of Buckingham. It was disafforested in 1630, and broken up for sale into small fee-farms. The peasantry were thus robbed of their ancient rights, and serious disturbances followed, during which a riotous assemblage of men and women, not being able to capture the Earl of Anglesea (whom they considered their prime enemy and oppressor), most ungallantly laid hands on his Countess, and carried off the noble lady prisoner.

Aubrey writes—" This Towne did stand in the Pewsham Forest. The Poore People have made this Rhyme;

>" When Chipnam stood
> In Pewsham's wood
> Before it was destroyed,
> A cowe might have gone for a groate a year,
> And now it is denyed."

He adds: "*The metre is lamentable, but the cry of the Poor was more lamentable.*"

Some compensation land, it was understood, after inclosure, was left on the sides of the highways for gardens and pasturage for the cottagers, but in course of years these tracts of land lying along the roadsides, often large and valuable, were swallowed up by landowners, under the plea that they were wastes of the Manor. This claim was wholly indefensible, the act absolutely illegal.

Two grand-daughters of the Earl of Anglesea, co-heiresses, having inherited Pewsham, the elder married into the Cary family, who, in 1791, sold the larger part to Mr. Montague, of Lackham, from whom it passed to the Lysleys. Elizabeth, the younger sister, was married to Lord Audley, and her portion of the Forest belongs to Mr. Ludlow Bruges.

Pewsham was formerly extra-parochial. It now forms a separate parish with Nethermore.

"MEM: Mr. Jo: Power told me heretofore that in Chippenham Forest was vitriol."   AUBREY.

Iron ore was once wrought in the Green Sand of Pewsham Forest.

"Upon the disafforestations the marterns (martens) were utterly destroyed in North Wilts. It is a pretty little beast, and of a deep chestnut colour, a kind of polecat, lesse than a fox; and the furre is much esteemed; not much inferior to sables."   AUBREY.

IV. GEOLOGY OF CHIPPENHAM.

CHIPPENHAM is situated between the oolite, the Cotswold Hills on one side, and the escarpment of the Chalk and Greensand on the other. All the north part of Wilts, from Cricklade to Trowbridge, seems, in ages long gone by, to have formed one large lake, and in later times, when a large volume of water had escaped through the Bradford chasm, several lakes were left in the lower grounds. The whole country from Tytherton to Dauntsey is a lake-bottom, lying upon gravel. This depression was dammed up by a ridge of Oxford clay. There is evidence of a pebble beach in Lackham woods.

The middle and lower part of the town are based on a limestone rock, on which the foundations of the Parish Church are laid, and which may be seen in its native character and undisturbed position, breaking out under the wall of the Churchyard, opposite the present Vicarage. This rock lies deep, is very hard, and yields but few fossils.

Eastwards and southwards, Chippenham rests on a bed of bluish clay, from 400 to 500 feet deep, through which, with very great labour, the Great Western Railway was cut; this formation extends to the base of Derry Hill, where it meets the sand, and thence spreads all over the lowlands of Pewsham.

The rich meadows enclosing the town, and furnishing finest loams for vegetation, are formed of alluvial soil of the latest fresh-water formations deposited on the limestone rock, and on clay, gravel, or blue marl.

On the west and north sides is the Inferior Oolite, stretching from Chippenham to Corsham and Box, where it joins the greater Oolite, the famous Bath Freestone; and on the north-west it passes on through Hardenhuish, Kington St. Michael and Stanton. This formation rests on a blue marl, which probably underlies the greater part of the surface of North Wilts.

A bed of iron sand-stone covers Bremhill, Derry, and Bowden Hills; stretching, with some alternations of the coralline strata to Devizes and Seend, where it is capped by the escarpments of the chalk.

A large bed of fossils, with rare Ammonites, is deposited in Peckingel Mead, in so solid a mass as to obtain a recognized place in the geological series, under the name of KELLAWAYS ROCK.

The appearance of a bituminous shale in the Oxford Clay has led to abortive sinkings for coal in this neighbourhood.

John Aubrey, himself a North Wiltshire-man, (born in the parish of Kington St. Michael), made the shrewd observation that the temperaments of the people in

North Wilts differed with the soils on which they lived —that the inhabitants on high, dry tablelands, were active, high-spirited, and intelligent, while those who lived on cold, damp, clayey soils, were heavy, slow, and impassive.*

"According to the several sorts of earth, the Indigenæ are respectively witty, or dull, good, or bad. In all changes of religion they are more zealous than any other; when in the time of the Rome-Catholique religion, there were more and better churches and religious houses founded than any other part of England can show, they are now the greatest fanatiques, even to spiritual madness. The rich, wet soil makes them hypocondricall.

"In North Wilts the Indigenæ, or Aborigines, speak drawling; they are phlegmatique, skins pale and livid, slow and dull, heavy of spirit; they live chiefly on milke meates, which cools their brains too much, and hurts their inventions. These circumstances make them melancholy, contemplative, and malicious, by consequence whereof come more law suites out of North Wilts, at least double to the Southern parts. And by the same reason they are more apt to be fanatiques: their persons are generally plump and feggy, gallipot eies and some black: but they are generally handsome enough. It is a woodsere country, abounding much with sowre and austere plants, as sorrel, &c. which makes their humours sowre.

---

* Felix Neff speaks of San Veran being the highest, and *consequently* the most pious village in the Italian Alps. It has been remarked also, by others, that there is a higher degree of religion in the elevated mountain hamlets of Piedmont than in the plain.

"Generally in the rich vales they sing clearer than on the hills, where they labour hard and breathe a sharp air.

"So in Somersetshire they generally sing well in the Churches; their pipes are smoother.

"In North Wilts the milkmayds sing as shrill and clear as any swallow." JOHN AUBREY, 1670.

V. *RIVER AVON, WELLS, AND SPRINGS.*

THE chief source of the Avon *(Afon,* a river, ? Saxon), is in the parish of Luckington, but it receives several brooks fed by the high lands sloping up to the Cotswold Hills. The soil out of which it springs is Cornbrash and Forest Marble, and over these Upper Oolitic strata the stream runs, for about eight miles, to Malmesbury, and thence by Broad Somerford, through Dauntsey Park, Christian Malford, and Kellaways to Chippenham, a course of thirteen miles. When Lord Carnarvon was asked why he did not build a mansion by the river side, in one of the rich meadows of Christian Malford (then his property), he said, " So I might, if I were an Ox."

For the first twenty seven miles of its course, the river flows through a series of valleys into an extensive plain of Oxford Clay, then through a channel between Chalk and Greensand, based on coral rag and calcareous grit, over gravel beds formed by the *debris* of rocks and the diluvium of its own silt.

Below Bradford it passes, for eight miles, over oolitic strata, through the valley of Bath, then, for twelve miles, towards Bristol, over lias, coal measures, and red sandstone, through the grand and tremendous chasm which cleaves the Magnesian Limestone at Clifton, over a flat of *alluvium;* and falls into the Severn at Avonmouth.

Its whole length is 73 miles, but a direct line drawn from its source to its mouth, would measure but 21 miles; its fall is trifling, as its current is sluggish. Its geological character is of much interest, for it can be said of the Wiltshire Avon (what perhaps cannot be said of any other river in England), that in its short course it washes the whole series of the Secondary strata. In the bed of this river was found the skull of a gigantic Ox, which testified to the existence of a race of colossal quadrupeds, whose bodies were twelve feet long, and six and half feet in breadth at the shoulders, ranging the vales of this district ages long ago.

Most of the freshwater fish common to English rivers are found in the Avon; Pike, Perch, Trout, Chub, Roach and Dace: the largest pike caught of late years weighed 20 lbs.; a perch was taken in this stream of 8 lbs, which is an extraordinary weight for this class of fish; very large eels come down with the floods, and are caught at the weirs.

The Avon first touches Chippenham parish, *(i e.,* the tithing of Tytherton*)* at the point where the rivulet, called Catbrook, separates Bremhill and Tytherton; thence it flows between the Peckingel Meads (in Langley Burrell) and West Tytherton, and near the Church is crossed by the Cradle Bridge.

William Woodruffe, a yeoman of Chippenham, by his will dated Sep. 1, 1664, gives to the Minister and Churchwardens of the parish of Kington St. Michael, (in which parish Peckingel was then situated), a rent charge of 30 shillings a year, "*in remembrance of God's mercies in preserving me in a wonderful manner from drowning at Peckingel Bridge,*" on 18 Sep. 1656, and the Minister is to preach a Sermon, and excite the people "*to be mindful of God's mercies, and to be thankful for the same.*"

Thence the stream flows westward, receiving the leat of old Tytherton Mill on the right, and the river Marden on the left, winds and meanders in pretty, picturesque reaches fringed with alders and rushes; encloses the town on the north in a horseshoe curve: passes Monkton Park (where it feeds an ancient pond called the Moat), turns the Old Town Mills, with a current separated into several artificial channels, passes under the Bridge of 21 arches, forms the Island of Ree, and other islets, flows by the Ivy, Rowden, and Lackham grounds, and dividing Pewsham from Lacock parish, makes a sweep to the east, and leaves Chippenham parish opposite Lackham House. The only part of the river which is safe for rowing is from Monkton to Peckingel.

The river MARDEN divides Chippenham parish from the tithing of Tytherton Lucas. It rises at the foot of Martinsell, or St. Ann's, Hill, near Marlborough. This hill gives birth also to the South Avon, which runs to Salisbury, and receiving the Wily falls into the sea at Christ Church, Hants, and to the Kennet, which flows by Marlborough and Hungerford into the Thames at Reading.

LOCKSWELL SPRING.

The Empress Maud granted to her Chamberlain, Drogo, certain land in Pewsham Forest. Drogo transferred the benefaction to a Cistercian brotherhood. On a hill in the Forest, a part of Drogo's gift, was a spring of the purest water, called "Lockswell," and the abbey which the monks built, bore the name of the "Abbey of Drogo's Fount," or "Drownfont." The water from this spring has flowed from time unknown, in a never failing, never varying volume of 150 gallons a minute.

"It is a magnificent spring, rising on the very top of the hill, which is on all sides surrounded with wild and romantic scenery. It appears in the spot in which it bursts, nearly three feet broad, singular and beautiful, rushing into day, and then winding its precipitous and solitary way till it is lost among the wildest glades of the ancient forest of Chippenham; once famous and hallowed, it has flowed for centuries through the wild bourne." BOWLES.

ON LOCKSWELL SPRING.

"Pure fount, that, welling from this wooded hill,
Dost wander forth, as into life's wide vale,
Thou to the traveller dost tell no tale
Of other years; a lone, unnoticed rill,
In thy forsaken tract, unheard of men,

Making thy own sweet music through the glen.
Time was when other sounds, and songs arose;
When o'er the pensive scene, at evening's close,
The distant bell was heard; or the full chant
At morn came sounding high and jubilant,
Or, stealing on the wildered pilgrim's way,
The moon light *Miserere* died away,
Like all things earthly—
　　　　　　　　Stranger, mark the spot—
No echoes of the chiding world intrude—
The structure rose, and vanish'd—solitude
　　　Possess'd the woods again—old Time forgot,
　　　Passing to wider spoil, its place and name,
Since then, ev'n as the clouds of yesterday,
Seven hundred years have well nigh pass'd away:
No wreck remains of all its early pride,
Like its own orisons its fame has died.
　　　But this pure fount, thro' rolling years the same,
Yet lifts its small still voice, like penitence,
Or lowly prayer. Then pass, admonish'd, hence,
Happy, thrice happy, if thro' good or ill,
Christian, thy heart respond to this forsaken rill,"
　　　　　　　　　　　　　　　BOWLES.

The sand hills give birth to many fine springs of water. At the foot of Derry Hill is a handsome well and canopy, inscribed with the following verses:

　　"Here quench your thirst, and mark in me
　　　An emblem of true charity,
　　　Who while my bounty I bestow

> Am neither seen nor heard to flow;
> Repaid by fresh supplies from heaven
> For every cup of water given."

Over a smaller spring and cistern at the top of the hill Canon Bowles caused this distich to be engraven:

> "Drink, traveller, and more than worldly wealth,
> Enjoy the best of earthly blessings, health."

A story goes that a traveller, weary and heated, parched with thirst, came to the spring, accepted the Canon's invitation, and imprudently took a long deep draught of the exceedingly cold water. He was seized with cholic and died. Soon after an epigram appeared, playing on the case:

> "Drink, drink," *quoth Bowles*
> *To thirsty souls,*
> "A fig for worldly wealth;
> This fountain clear
> Is pregnant here
> With the best of blessings, health."

and after summoning up the evidence given on the inquest, the solemn conviction was recorded that the poor traveller's death was caused by the couplet of Mr. Bowles:

> "Against whom was found
> On the clearest ground
> A verdict of manslaughter."

Aubrey speaks of "*Holy Well*," at Sheldon, and heard the water was "good for the eies."

ARTHUR'S WELL, on the Bath Road, has furnished for generations an inexhaustible supply of pure water.

In 1694 Judge Holland erected a vaulted building over a well in his garden, on the slope opposite Monkton Park, which was called "CHIPPENHAM SPA," and was supposed to be possessed of medicinal virtues. The fame of its waters as a fount of healing is gone, but part of the ornamental structure remains.

A copious spring of water rises in one of the islets in the river near the Bridge. In 1864, the use of this water was granted to the Town by the owner of Monkton.

Sir John Neeld gave 100 guineas for carrying the water under the bed of the river, to a basin placed at the end of the street, as high as the water would rise. On an iron plate above the fountain the following record is affixed:

MONKTON SPRING

"This water was given to the town of Chippenham by G. M. Esmeade, Esq.: and the expense of conveying it to this spot was defrayed by Sir John Neeld, Bart.

JAMES WHARRY, MAYOR, 1864."

VI. THE GARDEN OF WILTS.

CHIPPENHAM stands in the midst of the GARDEN OF WILTS. A circle drawn round the Old Town Hall, with a radius of five miles, encloses the finest scenery in the County. There is a very fine view from the brow overlooking Westmead, with the winding stream of the river in the foreground and expansive woodlands to the southward and eastward. In the grounds of the "Ivy House," adjoining the town, are to be seen some noble specimens of American trees, the Tulip tree, the Plane, the Maple, and Robinia (pseudo-Acacia), imported direct from North America by Mr. Northey.

Aubrey speaks (1690), as if there were in his possession a picture—"The Prospect of the Borough of Chippenham,"—which he hoped might be engraved with "*remarkable houses and prospects.*" He thought "*it would make a glorious volume.*" But it was never done.

A wide-spread field of natural beauty and diversified scenery is visible from Hardenhuish Churchyard.

The Birds' Marsh (anciently Birch Marsh), in the parish of Langley Burrell, with its glades and shady bowers, and labyrinths of evergreens, beds of anemones, daffodils, foxgloves, bluebells, and thickets of ferns, crowned with clusters of gorgeous rhododendrons, is a very paradise of loveliness and delight.

There used to be a breed of small yellow vipers in the Marsh, which were dangerous to the cattle feeding there; but not one reptile of this venomous species has been seen for many years.

The English snake is very common there, and is perfectly harmless. A lover of nature, cautiously observant, on a fine summer's day, may come upon a brood of snakelets at play with their mother in the sun, and may notice, how at the first signal of alarm, they glide into their mother's mouth, and all instantly disappear.

A vixen fox was seen hovering about a hedgerow, near the farm house, and a vigilant watch was kept over the poultry; but none were ever missed. Time went on, and all was peace; when, one evening, four or five cubs were noticed gambolling with their mother. But no turkey, or goose, or duck, or fowl was ever stolen from yard or field. It was evident that a compact had been made and respected—the farmer did not molest the fox; the fox did not rob the farmer. Yet foxes must be fed; and one day, a hare, a rabbit, and a fowl were seen in the cubs' larder. But they were brought from afar. The friend's property was not invaded. There is honour even among foxes.

A pair of missel-thrushes had built their nest in a tree near a spot where a peculiar fungus grew, which the birds regarded as delicate food. But a pair of squirrels also had found out this savoury meat, and used to sit upon the broad head of the fungus on their haunches, and nibble the edges. These thrushes, the boldest of birds, (fearing neither hawk nor owl) flew down and made pertinacious attacks on the little quadrupeds, fighting and scolding and pecking, and tugging at their tails, and striking them with their strong wings. The defenders of the position maintained their ground gallantly, springing at the assailants, hissing, and barking like little dogs, till at last they were driven off the fungus,—but the battle was not over; the nimble squirrels ran up the tree in which the birds had built, and took possession of their nest. The thrushes now flew to the defence of their home, and after a long fight they dislodged the enemy, but the squirrels ran down and again ensconced themselves upon the fungus; and thus the attack and defence went on till both parties were fairly tired out.

The Birds' Marsh was once a part of Langley Common. Langley Common was a free pasturage of eighty acres, given by generous grant of Saxon nobles, or, immediately, by the King himself, to the villagers of Langley Burrell and to the inhabitants of the Royal Burgh of Chippenham. That Chippenham was included in the grant is certain from the large extent of land conceded to common use.

In the beginning of the reign of Edward VI. A.D. 1547, there was in England a great demand for wool;

sheep were very valuable, and pasture was more profitable than tillage. The courtiers and county gentlemen, under grants from the Government, enclosed wastes and commons, for feeding sheep, so that the peasantry, driven out of their ancient heritages, were reduced to misery; and it was said *"A sheep is a more ravenous beast than lion or wolf, and devours whole parishes."*

Formidable insurrections broke out in England and Wales; and the Protector Somerset, whose influence in the Court was on the wane, countenanced the complaints of the dispossessed commoners, and issued a proclamation that the lands lately enclosed should be again laid open. The populace, thus encouraged, rose tumultuously in several counties, demolished fences and walls, and repossessed themselves of their ancient commons, downs, and woods. Sir William Herbert, who had just received the grant of the possessions of Wilton Abbey, hasted into Wales, raised a levy of wild mountaineers, and urged by tidings that the mob at Wilton had broken into his new park, marched rapidly into Wilts with his troopers, attacked the masses of countrymen in detail, and cut them up with such merciless severity, that from north to south the county trembled at his name.

Thus Langley Common was lost to Chippenham, on the north, much about the same time and in the same manner, that Pewsham Forest was lost on the south. They were the two lungs of Chippenham—both irreparable losses.

Langley Common fell (it is hardly known how) into the hands of certain proprietors who had obtained grants of pasturage, called Leazes, which became freehold, and gave rights of franchise. But as yet it was open. Other commons were sold, and enclosed.

Langley Common, though no longer free to the peasantry for grazing cattle, yet remained a noble, unincumbered area of eighty acres; cold, and bleak it was, especially when the winterly blasts swept down from the east,[*] but there were no obstacles of hedges, ditches, or stiles; all the old paths remained; it was free for breezy and bracing exercises, for riding, driving, and walking, and the youths of Chippenham played football, cricket, prisoners' base, and all manner of old English games of health and manliness wherever they pleased, unmolested and undebarred, as they had done for eight hundred years. But there came a fatal time, in the year 1838, when, under the Enclosure Act, a scheme was elaborated for enclosing Langley Common. It is true all the proceedings then taken to this end were illegal. The Commissioners had no power to enclose a Common within a certain distance of a town, with a certain population. Langley Common was within a mile of Chippenham, and Chippenham had a population of more than 5000 inhabitants.

---

[*] When the Mail-coach from the west, bringing up the Students to Oxford, reached the brow of Langley Common, the driver used to shout—"*Now, gentlemen, hold on your hats, for this is the windiest point between Exeter and Oxford.*"

But no protest was made: no hand uplifted to stem the ruin. Either through ignorance of the law, or through apathy, or from fear, the people of Chippenham silently acquiesced in the robbery, and whatever was left of their ancient right over Langley Common was lost for ever. Fortunately the ancient pathways, in the main, were not seriously interfered with, but gates, ditches, fences, and wretched stiles barred the traveller's way in all directions.*

The County Council of Wilts have done well in taking under their protection public paths; and it will be a worthy action, if they watch with a jealous eye the rights of ways across the country, resist any invasion of them, and insist on landowners fulfilling their legal responsibilities in keeping ancient paths in order, of providing fit footbridges, and convenient stiles.

Though Langley Common, as it has been said, was within the last sixty years, open to the youths for games, *not a foot of their ancient heritage can now be obtained, even by payment for it.* To the shame of the landowners of the Common be it spoken!—And it would be to the praise of the County Councillor for Langley, if he would move the Council to provide, by the compulsory powers which they possess of purchase or rental, for the boys of the neighbourhood, a sufficient piece of the Common, say four or five acres,

---

* "Sir," said an old countryman to a squire busy in obstructing the ancient tracks—"remember that *our* paths were here ages and ages before *your* hedges and ditches were made."

which justice and health (or if they prefer their new word *Hygiene*) alike demand. On the north side of the Common stands the shattered trunk of a huge elm, four hundred years old, which in its prime must have been the finest tree in the county.

Leaving Langley Burrell, its aged elms, its venerable Church, and secluded Churchyard, let the pilgrim of nature in search of the picturesque proceed towards Langley Fitzurse; and as soon as he enters that parish he finds (instead of the road over Langley Burrell Common compressed between stifling hedges) an open highway bounded by grassy wastes, 10 to 40 feet wide—they are parts of Langley Fitzurse Common; and "*hereby hangs a tale.*"

The Common includes 30 acres, and round it are planted farms, cottages and gardens, fringing the edge of the plateau, and forming one of the prettiest and healthiest villages in Wilts. To the westward lies a level plain extending through Gloucestershire to the Cotswold; the views, south and east, present, as Aubrey says, "*a delicate prospect,*" over wooded lowlands, of the hills of Bremhill and Bowood, Cherhill Downs and Salisbury Plain.

The Common is the glory of Langley Fitzurse. But it narrowly escaped in 1860 the fate which befell its neighbour at Langley Burrell in 1838.

A plot was concocted—maps and plans were prepared —sections were laid out for partition and enclosure— and *on paper* the thing was done. But as soon as the design was breathed, it awakened a storm of vehement indignation; acting under legal counsel, the people stood on their rights, and threatened uncompromising hostility to the bitter end ——— And the project for enclosure was silently abandoned.

Thus the Common was saved for that day. But it behoves the parishioners of Langley Fitzurse to look well to their interests for the future.

Draycot Park is intersected by public paths to Seagry and Stanton which may be trodden without fear of prosecution. In the silent solitude of this Park, (though small,) nature may be studied in all its wildness. The growth of the ferns is grand; Aubrey in his day remarked "*they are the biggest and tallest I ever saw, as high about as a man on horseback.*" That part called "Scotland," with its old weird death-struck oaks, seems like a veritable *relique* of the ancient forest.

The extent and variety and colouring of the landscape of the GARDEN OF WILTS cannot be embraced, or sufficiently admired, except when seen from the undulating heights which enclose and command it.

From Charlcot there is a drive (open to the public by permission of Lord Lansdowne), which winds around the brow of the hills to Maud Heath's pillar on Wick Hill, and thence to Bencroft, which opens to the enraptured eye a magnificent expansion of heaven above and earth below; but this scene, to be thoroughly appreciated, should be visited on a clear day after rain.

Of Bowood we may simply adopt the *dictum* of John

Aubrey about Wilton:—"*The situation of Bowood is incomparably noble. It hath the most pleasant prospect of the gardens and park. The house is great and august; but I attempt no further description of the house, gardens, and approaches, as falling too short of the greatness and excellency of it.*"

And no language can describe the beauty of the scenery near and far, from Derry Hill, Lockswell, Nethermore, and Bowden Hill, especially when, in mid-autumn, the Lord of Creation is painting his superb pictures on the wide-stretched canvas of earth and sky, in colours of yellow, brown, amber, orange, and red, the rich hues of the departing glory of the dying leaf.

But——there may be scenery of surpassing loveliness; hills, woods, rivers, valleys; there may be foliage of every tint; a sky of spotless azure, a glowing sun, balmy breezes——but these do not make heaven—— or else a heaven may be found in many parts of the "GARDEN OF WILTS."

> "O GOD, oh good, beyond compare!
> If thus Thy earthly works are fair—
> If thus Thy glories gild the span
> Of ruined earth and sinful man;
> How glorious must the mansions be
> Where Thy redeemed shall dwell with Thee!"
>
> BISHOP HEBER.

It is deeply to be regretted that, in this day, eminent men, who are justly celebrated for their profound research into natural science have failed to see and acknowledge in all their astonishing discoveries the hand and mind of an Omniscient, Omnipresent Creator; —have not "*looked up from Nature unto Nature's* God." A very different man to these philosophers was the great Swedish botanist, Linnæus—the more deeply he penetrated into the secrets of Nature, the more he magnified the work of the mighty Master; whenever he had opportunity (which often happened in his lectures and botanical excursions) he expatiated on the greatness, the goodness, the wisdom, the providence, the presence of God; his heart glowed with celestial fire, his tongue poured forth torrents of adoring admiration.

Of Joseph Alleine, (born at Devizes, in the troublous times of Charles I.), it is recorded—"*He did often in his devotions delight to converse with the fowls of the air, and the beasts of the field; with streams and plants he did delight to talk; and all these did utter to his attentive ear the praise and knowledge of the great Creator.*"

> "Thou, who hast given me eyes to see and love this
>   sight so fair,
> Give me a heart to find out Thee, and read Thee
>   everywhere."   KEBLE.

When John Evelyn was visiting Sir Edward Baynton at Spye Park in 1652, he pronounced that the house was built "on the precipice of an *incomparable* prospect"——and who a better authority on the characteristics of the true picturesque than the author of "Sylva."?*

* John Evelyn wrote "Sylva, a Discourse on Forest Trees," in 1664. Within a few years millions of oaks, elms, and ashes, were

With the *Ipse Dixit* of John Evelyn and a Poem of Canon Bowles, we leave the GARDEN OF WILTS.

SKETCH FROM BOWDEN HILL.

" How cheering are thy prospects, airy hill!
      How rich,
How mantling in the gay and gorgeous tints
Of summer! Far beneath me, sweeping on
From field to field, from vale to cultured vale,
The prospect spreads its crowded beauties wide;
Long lines of sunshine, and of shadow, streak
The farthest distance: where the passing light
Alternate falls, 'mid undistinguished trees,
White dots of gleaming domes, and peeping towers,
As from the painter's instant touch, appear.
  As thus the eye ranges from hill to hill,
Here white with passing sunshine, there with trees
Innumerable shaded, clustering more
As the long vale retires, the ample scene,
Warm with new grace and beauty, seems to live.
Lives! all is animation! beauty! hope!
   O Nature thee, in the soft winds,
Thee, in the soothing sound of summer leaves,
When the still earth lies sultry; thee, methinks,
Ev'n now I hear bid welcome to thy vales
And woods again!

planted in Great Britain. To this date, (and probably to this book,) we owe the stately timber trees which now so grandly adorn the GARDEN OF WILTS.

HISTORY OF CHIPPENHAM.

          And I will welcome them,
And pour, as erst, the song of heartfelt praise.
From yonder line, where fade the farthest hills
Which bound the blue lap of the swelling vale,
On whose last line, seen like a beacon, hangs
Thy tower,* benevolent, accomplished Hoare!
To where I stand, how far the interval.
Yet instantaneous to the hurrying eye
Displayed, though peeping towers and villages,
Thick scattered, 'mid the intermingling elms,
And towns remotely marked by hovering smoke,
And grass green pastures with their herds, and seats
Of rural beauty, cottages, and farms,
Unnumbered as the hedgerows, lie between.

    Beaming at large to where the gray sky bends,
The eye scarce knows to rest, till back recalled,
By yonder ivied cloisters† in the plain,
Whose turret, peeping pale above the shade,
Smiles in the venerable grace of years.

          O venerable pile! though now no more
The pensive passenger at evening hears
The slowly-chanted vesper, or the sounds
Of "*Miserere*" die along the vale,
Yet piety and honoured age‡ retired
There hold their blameless sojourn, ere the bowl
Be broken, or the silver cord be loosed.

    * Stourton Tower, built by Sir R. C. Hoare.
        † Lacock Abbey.
The aged Countess of Shrewsbury, then residing in the Abbey.

     Nor can I pass
Without a secret prayer that so my age
In charity and peace may wait its close.
    Yet still be with me, O delightful friend,
Soothing companion of my vacant hours,
Oh, Spirit of the Muse, to animate
And warm my heart, whene'er the prospect smiles,
With all the works of GOD. So cheer my path,
From youth to sober manhood, till the light
Of evening smile upon the fading scene.
    And though no pealing clarion swell my fame,
When all my days are gone—let me not pass
Like the forgotten clouds of yesterday;
Nor unremembered by the fatherless
Of the loved village where my bones are laid."*

---

 * Canon Bowles was Vicar of Bremhill, but he was buried in the Cloisters of Salisbury Cathedral.

VII. STANLEY ABBEY.

STANLEY ABBEY was located in the extreme eastern angle of Chippenham Forest, on the southern bank of the Calne Water; the Church and Monastery were within the parish of Bremhill, but their lands extended far into Chippenham Parish.

Lockswell, in the south of Pewsham Forest, had been conferred by Henry, Duke of Normandy, and Maud the Empress, on her chamberlain, Drogo; this nobleman, or his immediate representatives, transferred the estate to a House of Cistercian monks, who settled at Lockswell in 1151, and laid the foundations of an Abbey, close to the famous springs. On receiving an additional grant of meadow land in the valley, after a three years' residence on the hills, the monastic household migrated to Stanley. The solidity and breadth of the walls in Lockswell Abbey Farm-house make it highly probable that they are remains of the old conventual building: and the reservoir also, below the house, in its original construction, must have been due to the labours of the monks.

The Abbot, no doubt, went down to Stanley, because of its sheltered situation, in rich pastures, and beside a river, where the monks could form fish ponds, and build a mill, an indispensable boon to them and their peasantry. Their mill is working still, and the abutment of a bridge they built was remaining sixty years ago; but the glorious Abbey Church they raised, and their magnificent monastery have perished to their very foundations.

The Abbey was called *Stanleia Imperatricis*, because the Empress Maud granted the endowment; but what they gained in good land the brotherhood had lost in good water. So by a bold venture they determined to convey the pure fresh stream at Lockswell through an underground conduit from the source of the spring to the site of the new Abbey, at Stanley, a distance of three miles. A manuscript in the Bodleian records that "*In the year 1214 the aqueduct was finished by Thomas de Colestune* (Colston) *the Abbot, who, though "timide incepit"*—he began in fear—*yet "Deo et Domino Jesu Christo sibi auxiliante"*—by the help of God and the Lord Jesus Christ—*he successfully completed this good and noble work, for which his memory ought to be blessed for ever.*" The aqueduct must have been of stone. The tradition of its existence is still firm; portions have been broken into, large enough to admit a boy.

Edward I. gave 211 acres in Nethermore; his charter first mentions the rivulet Pewe, which gives its name to the district. That King also granted a license to the Abbot "*fodiendi mineralia ferri*"—to dig iron in the Forest. Richard I. added Hedfield, near the

Forest of Chippenham—"*dominium nostrum cum septem homnibus ibi manentibus*" *i.e.* seven farms with their tenants—on both sides of the Avon, and of "dead wood in the forest as much as they want for fires; and timber when needed for their buildings to be taken in view of the Forester; also pasture and pannage, free and quiet, for the pigs of the Seven men, and for their own pigs, animals, and flocks." Richard II. gave lands and tenements in Chippenham, Langley Burrell, Cockleborough, Allington, Estmeade, &c.; and "*threepence a day are to be paid for ever out of our Farm of Chippenham as long as Stanley shall be inhabited by Religious Folk.*"

The Church was dedicated by Walter de Wyle, Bishop of Sarum, in 1266.

Canon Bowles writes—"*The wild forests of Wiltshire, as well as the vast swamps in other Counties, were reclaimed by these ascetic inmates of the cloister, and the moorlands they brought into cultivation are now the most productive lands in the county.*" Again he says—"*The taper of learning in the solitary cloister was the only one that cast any light at that benighted period. The hum of industry and the voice of prayers were heard, by turns, wherever they fixed their abode. The fate of these sumptuous establishments sometimes moves a sigh when we recollect the early industry they promoted; the learning and piety they encouraged; and also the charities they dispensed. But they were smitten in their pomp and pride; and the monastic system, containing, amid many gross impurities and impieties, much which the sincerest piety might approve, and much that charity might forgive, for ever passed away.*"

Very few written memoranda of Stanley Abbey remain.

Fulke Fitzwarine, a scion of one of the fiercest and proudest of the Norman families, while playing with Prince John, (son of Henry II.) when a mere boy, checkmated him in a game of chess. Whereupon in a passion John snatched up the chessboard, and struck the young Norman on the head. His blood boiled up, and he returned the assault with such vigour, that the Prince fell against the wall, struck his head, and lay senseless. As soon as he recovered he ran sobbing to his father. The King told him he richly deserved what he had got; sent for his tutor, and ordered him to flog the boy, (as the romance of Fitzwarine words it) "*finely and well.*" John never forgot the affront. As soon as he was King, he seized all Fulke's estates. Fulke armed his followers, and aided by other barons, who smarted under John's tyranny, carried on a petty warfare against the Sovereign. His adventures and escapes in many a county of England would make a long tale. Once in North Wilts, when in ambush in Braden Forest, news reached him of the approach of a party of merchants bearing rich cloths and other valuable goods purchased in foreign parts for the King and Queen. Fitzwarine pounced on them, and divided the costly brocades, silks, and ermines among his soldiers—then released the merchants, and sent his compliments to their Majesties for their acceptable present. John was soon on his track, and hunted him from place to place, till in his desperate necessity, he ran to sanctuary in Stanley Abbey. "*Here he was besieged,*" says a Latin MS. in the Bodleian) *fourteen days by almost all the County of Wilts, but came out safe in the peace of the Church, and was reconciled in the following year,* 1202." In the time of Edward II., the Earl of Hertford, Roger Mortimer, Audley, and other of Queen Isabella's adherents, forced a violent entrance into Stanley Abbey, and seized the treasures of Hugh de Spencer deposited with the Abbot for safety; they broke open his coffers, and carried off £1000 in money, besides cups of gold and silver, jewels, charters, muniments and letters.

In 1536, amongst the many consecrated retreats which had served in their earlier day the cause of learning, hospitality and charity, and might under proper regulations have been instrumental to the same holy purposes to this day,* "the hideous Henry smote to the dust" Stanley Abbey.

The site and part of the lands were sold by the King to Sir Edward Baynton, 14 Feb, 1537, for £1200:

---

* Bishop Latimer, in his honest earnestness, implored the King to spare two or three monasteries or convents in every shire, to be true homes of the religious life, into which men and women, aged, sick, sad, friendless, nauseating the world, might retire for awhile, and commune with GOD, and so prepare for—

> That inevitable day,
> When a voice to me shall say,
> "Thou must rise, and come away—
> All thy other journeys past,
> Gird thee, and make ready fast,
> For thy longest, and thy last."
>
> TRENCH.

they descended to the Starkeys, of Spye Park, who had intermarried with the Bayntons. The site of the Abbey now is possessed by the Marquis of Lansdowne.

Some encaustic tiles and sculptured stones were collected by Canon Bowles, and are preserved in an oratory in the vicarage garden at Bremhill, "*the last asylum,*" as he says, "*of their departed splendour and perished fortunes.*"

The south wall of the old farm house built in the Abbey grounds, (now itself falling into ruins), displays stones and oaken beams which may belong to the original erection; carven stones of ecclesiastical character lie here and there; here is a stone coffin, there are numberless fragments of tiles, beautifully patterned in still fresh colours, betokening the site of the Church; the local situation of the monastic buildings (which served as a quarry for 200 years) is shown by depressions in the meadow; the venerable font, used in the Church for 400 years, desecrated for 350 years, stands now upon a solid cross of freestone on the lawn of the new farm house. These ancient, holy relics awaken solemn memories.

Three Kings of England are recorded as having each passed a night at Stanley Abbey; John, Edward I., and Edward II.

The Society consisted of only thirteen White Monks, but the lay brothers, officials, servitors, and labourers might have numbered one hundred. Their annual revenue at the Dissolution was £222 14s. 4d.

During the making of the Calne Railway, which passed through the Abbey lands, 12 or 14 skeletons were unearthed, lying face downwards; and seven feet below the surface a blacksmith's forge was discovered, with small coal quite fresh.

VIII. CHIPPENHAM PARISH.

THE Parish of Chippenham include the tithings or townships of West Tytherton, Stanley, and Nethermore. Detached portions formerly lay in Kington St. Michael, Langley Burrell, and elsewhere, and parts of other parishes were enclosed within the limits of Chippenham parish; but by the Divided Parishes Act each parish is now contained by a continuous line.

The parish of Chippenham proper is bounded on the north by Yatton Keynell, Kington St. Michael, Hardenhuish, and Langley Burrell; east by Tytherton; south by Pewsham; west by Biddestone.

The area of the old parish was 6981 acres: 14 acres are glebe; the Church Trustees hold 1a. 2r. 26p.; the Corporation own 126a. 0r. 34p.; and 42a. belong to the Great Western Railway Company, not including the Calne Branch. Stanley is bounded by Tytherton, Bremhill, the Liberty of Bowood, Pewsham, and Chippenham; Nethermore by Chippenham, Pewsham, Bowood, Bishop's Cannings, Bromham, and Lacock. Under recent legislation Nethermore was separated from Chippenham and united with Pewsham.

Though Pewsham Forest was considered to be included in Chippenham Forest, yet the parish of Pewsham was never a part of Chippenham parish. Pewsham contained 1296 acres, but had no ecclesiastical existence, being without Church, Vicar, and Vestry, yet it paid tithes.

The area of Chippenham parish is now 6191 acres; by the abstraction of the whole of Nethermore with portions of Langley Burrell, Hardenhuish, and Kington St. Michael, its ancient content was reduced by 790 acres.

THE BOROUGH.

Chippenham is now ruled by a Mayor, Aldermen, and Councillors, but as a municipal power these officers are very young, having been created under the Corporations Reform Act in 1854. Before that time the Town was governed by a Bailiff and Twelve Burgesses, whose title to a Corporate Body rested upon a Charter granted by Queen Mary.

The records of the borough (now in the custody of the Corporation) throw no light on the early history of the government of Chippenham, as they do not begin till 1554. But Chippenham was a Borough by prescription, and governed by a Bailiff for many hundred years before Queen Mary granted her charter. Ever since it was a part of the Royal Desmesne, it was under the charge of some representative of the Crown. Sometimes this official was called Steward, as at Calne; sometimes Portreeve, as at Great Bedwyn; but his appellation at Bromham, Corsham, Chippenham, and Melksham, was Bailiff. As this officer was commissioned to protect the Royal interests, he was armed originally with formidable powers (being second only to the King himself within the Manor), for he had at his command not only a prison and pillory, but also a gallows, and a hangman too.

But after the Manor was subdivided into several royalties, each carrying semimanorial rights, owners of lands granted by the Crown, and sometimes the superior Crown officers, questioned and counteracted the authority of the Bailiff. During the reign of Henry III. Robert Stoket, Bailiff of Chippenham, seized some packs of wool passing through the town; the Sheriff of Wilts ordered him to restore them. A fellow, imprisoned in the castle of Old Sarum, had turned "King's Evidence," and had implicated in his charge one "Solomon the Jew," of Chippenham. The Sheriff of Wilts issued his warrant to the Bailiff of Chippenham (Robert Stoket) to arrest the Jew, but, before the warrant was served, Godfrey Gascelyn, lord of the manor, dared the Bailiff to take any proceedings till he had communicated with the Sheriff. Meanwhile Solomon disappeared. One Nicholas Hamund, who had been sent to prison by the Bailiff, was released by the Sheriff.

It was evident, that for the peace of the town, the true powers of the Chief Officer should be defined, and that he should be confirmed in his local authority. Therefore a petition was presented to Queen Mary at the beginning of her reign that she would grant the borough a new charter, and she, desirous of ingratiating herself with her subjects, conferred both a charter and a grant of land.

THE CHARTERS.

The Charter of Queen Mary is dated May 2nd, 1554; it runs thus ——

On petition of the inhabitants of the Town and Borough of Chippenham for the better government thereof, and for the advantage of being incorporated into one body politic, the Queen decrees that the said Town and Borough shall be a free Borough for ever, of one Bailiff and Twelve Burgesses to form one body corporate: that they may plead and be impleaded, shall have a Common Seal, and may acquire lands; and the Borough shall extend from Brymland Lands, on the west, to the Yate post of Huntingdon Lands on the east; and from the midst of the Bridge of Chippenham on the north to Cook Street on the south; and she nominates Henry Farnewell (alias Goldney) to be the first Bailiff with twelve selected Burgesses, and that the Burgesses shall meet in the "Yelde Hall" (or other place) and elect a Bailiff on death, and shall make statutes for the Borough: and whereas for the maintenance of Two Burgesses at the Parliament, and for the reparations of a certain great bridge on the river Avon, and of a certain bank called a "Cawsaye," they are grievously burthened, her Majesty grants to the Town the

Pasture called Inglands, containing 17 acres, and Westmead, containing 30 acres, and one Messuage, and a moiety of one yardland and four parcels called "Poks" in Rowden's Down containing 120 acres, one close called Burleis containing 4 acres, and 21 acres of arable land in Chippenham Common Field, and a Wood called Rowden's Down Coppice, containing 21 acres, and Bolt's Croft, heretofore parcel of the lands of the late Lord Hungerford, to be Borough lands of Chippenham, and now of the yearly value of Nine Pounds, Twelve Shillings, and Eight Pence; and Two Burgesses shall be elected and sent to Parliament at the charge of the Borough.

LANDS GIVEN BY QUEEN MARY:

	ACRES.
INLANDS	17
WEST MEAD	30
POKES	120
BURLEYS	4
COMMON FIELD	21
ROWDEN DOWN COPPICE	21
BOLTS CROFT	4
	217

The history in connection with the conveyance of these lands is curious. It has been seen that no part of the Desmesne remained in the hands of the Crown in the time of Mary, except Pewsham Forest; and this district, being then covered with timber, would be of little value.

Very conveniently for the Queen, it happened that a few years before her accession, in the reign of Henry VIII., Walter Lord Hungerford, who held a large part of Chippenham parish, had been accused of High Treason for calling the King "a heretic," and for having suffered one William Byrd, Vicar of Bradford, in Wilts, to make experiments in alchemy, in his house, with a design of ascertaining how soon the King might die. For these acts of High Treason, Lord Hungerford lost his head on Tower Hill, and with his head lost all his manors in Chippenham, and many other goodly estates in Wilts, and elsewhere.

This property was all confiscated by the Crown. It was out of the forfeited lands of Lord Hungerford in Chippenham that Mary, (as advised) made her grants to the Borough. And the Charter was executed only just in time, for Walter, the heir of Lord Hungerford, came of age twenty three days after the deed received the Sign Manual, when he was restored in name, blood, and estate, by Act of Parliament.

Let it be remembered that Queen Mary did not create the Borough of Chippenham. Her Charter confirmed ancient Burgage privileges, franchises, and immunities granted by Saxon, Norman, and Plantagenet Sovereigns under legal deeds and instruments now lost.

Queen Elizabeth also granted a Charter "*Ballino et Burgensibus Burgi de Chippenham,*" but it only recites and confirms that of her Sister in every particular.

In 1574 a suit had been lodged in the Court of Chancery that "*the Towne lands, given for charitable purposes and the publique good, were misemployed unto the private benefit of some few of the incorporation,*" and Sir Walter Hungerford, Sir John Danvers, Sir Henry Sherrington, and John Eyre, Esq. made an award rectifying the abuses. In 1604, the Bailiff and some of the Burgesses prosecuted the other Burgesses and some of the inhabitants because they held that St. Mary's St. was not in the borough; Lord Chancellor Egerton recommended an amicable arrangement, and nominated certain Commissioners, who decided that St. Mary St. *was* in the borough, and who suggested "*for the extinguishing the miseries that daily grow out of strife and of the malice springing up between the inhabitants,*" certain ordinances to be binding on all the town.

Some of the lands given to the town by Queen Mary were afterwards discovered to be no part of Lord Hungerford's property, but to belong to the Crown, as " assart lands in Chippenham Forest," and were claimed by James I. On the payment of £40 they were secured to the Borough by the King's Letters Patent, which further confirmed to the Bailiff and Burgesses " all the lands, tenements, messuages, rents, rights, *aquas, piscaria, piscaciones;* waters, fishponds, fisheries "—which they and their predecessors had been accustomed to hold in any former time by grants of Kings or Queens of England.

LANDS SOLD TO THE CORPORATION OF CHIPPENHAM BY JAMES I, IN 1607.

	A.	R.	P.
INLANDS AND COT	26	3	11
BOLTS CROFT	5	0	20
WEST MEAD (rest of)	34	0	0
	65	3	32

also all the tithes great and small, with a reserved rent to the Crown of nine shillings.

Both Charles II. and James II., besides depriving cities and towns of their charters by legal compulsion, induced other boroughs voluntarily to surrender their rights, under a promise of a new charter with superior privileges.

An entry among the Borough Records is ominous as to the fate of the deeds and documents relating to the history and privileges of Chippenham from 1100 to 1554——

1685. "The former Charter granted by Queen Mary, *with divers other Charters of this Borough* was surrendered into the hands of Charles II., 1684."

The older Charters were never returned, and may be in existence still in the Record Office in London.

James the Second renewed the Charter, which the borough of Chippenham had surrendered, on Mar. 13, 1685, but with the proviso that the Privy Council might make or cancel all appointments, and under this clause he removed John Flower, Bailiff, and four Burgesses, and nominated William Bedford, and others, in their place. But alarmed by dark clouds gathering round the throne, he restored to Chippenham all its corporate privileges, and, it appears, he took the opportunity as he was passing through the town in 1687, to present the new Concession in person. The costs and the homage fees of £36 6s. 8d. were paid by Richard Kent, M.P. for the town.

THE TOWN HALL.

A few years ago two lonely, solemn, smoke-begrimed trees, (supposed to be evergreens) stood before a solemn, ancient, smoke-begrimed building with two small gables, surmounted by an old wooden turret on the east side of the Market Place of Chippenham.

1894. The trees are gone. The building remains. It is the Old Town Hall; the venerable Council Chamber of the Borough for centuries. It bears on its front the Borough Arms, and the letters "J.S. 1776."——probably the initials of John Scott, Bailiff, who repaired it that year.

When Walter Lord Hungerford was attainted, and all his estates were seized by Henry VIII., the attainder did not touch the heir, and the King assented to the restoration of all the confiscated property, except the Hundred and Manor of Chippenham, which he devised on certain grantees for life, "Roberte Serle and Laurence Wamsley," and made them Bailiffs of Chippenham; and afterwards conveyed it as a marriage portion to Queen Katharine Parr for her life. Edward VI., as has been mentioned, sold the fee to Lord Darcy, and he re-sold it to Sir W. Sherrington.

"In the midst of the street of the town stood a Yelde Hall or Churche House alone by it self from all other houses wch the Inhabitantes of the sayde towne time oute of mynde have Repaired and therein kepte their churche ales and plaies and have had their metynge for making of ordinances for the same towne &c. and in the same howse by the time the Lordes of the Hundrede have kepte theire Lawe daies and hundrede Courtes."

It was contended by the town that the patent of Edward VI. granting the Hundred never conveyed the freehold of the Yelde, or Guild, Hall to the grantee; though it seems, Lord D'Arcy, or his assigns, claimed it, and the dispute ran on for two hundred years.

Henry Sherrington, having succeeded to his father's property, and preparing vigourously to enforce his supposed rights in reference to the Town Hall of Chippenham, the Bailiff and Burgesses petitioned the Queen (Elizabeth) for protection.

The "Queen's Steward of the Town of Chippenham" wrote to the Lord Chief Justice, informing him that there had long been a variance between the Town of Chippenham and Mr. Sherrington "*by occasion of a graunt which he had obtained from the Prince,*" and sent a draft of the case. The Attorney General appears to have proceeded against Sherrington, but the Barons on hearing the suit, quashed the Information. Thus encouraged

"Henrie Sherington, Esquier, aboute St. Andrewes tide $vidl^t$ the third day of Noveb^r. in the ixth year of the Queenes ma^{ts} rayne that nowe is (1566) sent thre of his household servants wth staves and axes in riotous manner to the towne of Chipnam to cutt downe certen shambles and shoppes there whereupon one Thomas Asheley bocher one of the Tenants of Sr Walter Hungerford came wth a staffe and comaunded the said M^r. Sherringtons men to leave hewying downe of his shoppe for that he had his vittell there and two of his boies lyeing in the shoppe to keepe the possession thereof the dore beyng Locked and the windowes fast, they annswered they would not whereupon the saide Thomas Ashley owner of the shoppe kepyng the possession thereof and seying they would not cease to hewe downe his shoppe did strike at one of M^r. Sher-.ingtons men and they strake at him agayne and thereupon came the Balie of the towne and the constables to kepe the queenes peace and to putt them asunder, at wch time one John Croke one of M^r. Sheringtons men did take one Laurence Madocke constable of the towne by the bosome and askte him what he had to doo wth the matter whoo aunswered that he came to see the queenes peace kept. Then the saide Thomas Asheley and one Richard Vyncent required the said Bailie and constables that they wold arest the said M^r. Sheringtons men of the peace, whereupon the Bailie and constables required M^r. Sheringtons men to go to M^r. Edward Baynton justice of peace, wch M^r. Baynton hearyng the matter of bothe parts, willed them not to take the peace one of another for that it wold be chardge to both parts, and thereupon tooke uppe the matter and so they departed wth oute anie further punyshement."

To the wise suggestion of the magistrate both parties at first agreed. Afterwards Sherrington brought an action against the Bailiff and constable for arresting his servants without a warrant, and when he was Sheriff of Wilts in the same year (1566), he arrested both the officers "with a *latitat*, and wold take no Baile, but sent them to the comon Jayle," and kept the key of the "churche house of Chipnam called the yeild hall, and dothe clayme it to be his inheritance as parcell of the hundrede." But, probably weary of the strife, in 1569, Sherrington leased his tolls of Fairs and Markets within the borough to the Bailiff and Burgesses, and their successors, for 40 years, at a rent of £8 a year, they covenanting to keep the Hall in repair, and allow the lord of the Hundred to keep his Law day there once in the year, and to provide "one convenient and sufficient Dynner" for the Steward and his servants.

Up to this time the Guild Hall had stood alone on a vacant spot of ground on the east side of the Market Place. Now, in 1580, leases were granted to erect stalls, shambles, and shops, and all other buildings, fit and expedient for fairs and markets, in and upon the Market Place, and other waste and void places. Hither converged all the trade of the town, and besides public houses and butchers' shambles, shops were built by a 'weaver,' 'mercer,' 'lynnen draper,' 'clothman,' 'carrier,' 'cordwainer,' &c.

The Quarter Sessions were held in the Town Hall, when the floor was strewn with herbs and green rushes, (at a cost to the Borough of *eightpence)*, and perfumed with frankincense, resin, and pitch (at a cost of *fourpence*), and adorned "with certain stuffe to hang about the Hall when the Justices sat"—the "stuffe" was borrowed of Sir Gilbert Prynne at Allington House, and it cost *sixpence* for carriage.

The dues of the Hundred, apart from the rents of the Shambles, amounted to £40 a year.

In 1568 Nicholas Snell, by warrant of the Earl of

Pembroke, High Steward of Chippenham, kept Lawday in the Yeld Hall.

This old Hall, built about 400 years ago, though often repaired and beautified, is little altered from its original construction, and demands honourable and reverential treatment from the people of Chippenham. A good painting of the Royal Arms of Elizabeth, A.D. 1594, which once adorned its walls, now hangs in an anteroom of the New Hall. That part of the Shambles, which was destroyed in 1892, certainly ought to have been preserved, as unique, and a very ancient, and most interesting relic of old Chippenham.

MEMBERS OF PARLIAMENT.

The first true Parliament of England was summoned by Edward I. in 1295. To it he cited by writ the Barons, Bishops, Knights of Shires, and Burgesses of Boroughs. These formed the three Estates of the Realm—Clergy, Lords, and Commons; and to this Parliament were elected for the Borough of Chippenham Johannes de Burle and Robertus Osgode. On many occasions, and for long intervals, the privilege remained in abeyance, and for some Parliaments no returns for Chippenham can be found; but from the year A.D 1295 to A.D. 1865, through 570 revolving years, Chippenham was privileged to send two members to the British Parliament.

The names of about 88 M.P's (allowing for those whose names are illegible, or torn off the Roll) remain as representatives of Chippenham through the Plantagenet, Lancastrian, Yorkist, and Tudor reigns, till I Mary—and from the date of Mary's first Parliament, Sep. 10, 1553 (to which Robartus Wrastly and Henricus Farnewell, *alias* Goldney, were elected for Chippenham), through the reigns of the Stuart and Hanoverian Sovereigns, during which the lists are absolutely perfect, except for 1654 and 1656, (when no returns appear) about 160 Burgesses have represented the Borough of Chippenham.

Many of these men were famous in their day in the County of Wilts, and some have left a mark on the page English history.

Hungerford and Baynton occur again and again throughout the seventeenth century—Popham—Hyde—Eyre—Speke—Talbot—Montague—Lord Mordaunt—Long, often and often—Rolt—Eyres—Holland, *et al.*

In early times the Burgesses elected to Parliament were paid for their time and labours by their constituents. It will be noted that one express purpose of Q. Mary giving land to the Borough, was to meet the great cost of maintaining two Burgesses of Parliament. In the middle ages Knights for the Shire received 4 shillings, and Burgesses for the Borough 2 shillings a day, by warrant of the Crown. Money would be worth ten times what it is now. All travelling was then on horseback, and the animals were as heavy as carthorses. Parliament was not always held in London; it followed the King to York, Reading, or elsewhere; and the dangers and expense of these journeys were very great. It took 4 or 5 days to ride from Chippenham to London, and the roads (only rugged lanes) over the Wiltshire Downs, which was the shortest way, were infested with robbers.

" Salisbury Plain, Salisbury Plain,
Never without a thief or twain."

Fathers of Chippenham before leaving home made their wills, and took solemn farewell of their families, as though they would never see them again.

But in time the noble public thought 2 shillings a day too high a payment for their representative's service, and reduced "his wages" to 1 shilling a day. At Dunwich, on the Essex Coast, which was famous for herrings, the electors made a composition with their "sitting member," viz. that

"Whether the Parliament hold long time or short, or whether it fortune to be prorogued, he will take for his wages "a barrel and half of herrings."

Chippenham was famous for the manufacture of fine broad cloth—there is not any evidence to show whether this borough presented their M. P's for their wages a suit of clothes, surcoat, waistcoat, knee-breeches, and pantaloons. But there is evidence that in 1603, when John Hungerford and John Roberts were elected, " 94 *householders were taxed at* 12d *apiece, and* 92 *inhabitants at* 8d *apiece, wages for John Robarts, a burgess for Parliament, for* 17 *weeks, viz.* 120 *days at* 2/- *a day."*

The Members of Parliament were always elected in

the Old Town Hall. If its walls could hear and speak, it would tell some startling tales about contested elections, and tumultuous nominations, and vehement declamations, and excited pollings, and unblushing bribery, and broken pledges, and disappointed hopes, and savage fights.

The question was once asked——"*How many voters are there in Chippenham, and what would be the probable cost of an election?*"

It was answered——"*There are 129 burgage houses in the borough, (the same number it is supposed as when Mary's grant was made) and each house has a vote, but only 102 will vote now, as 27 are occupied by widows or maidens. Every freeman expects at least £10 for his vote. A sum of between £3000 and £4000 must be deposited with responsible Trustees. The dinner will cost £500; the supper and ball, two days after, £500. The last successful candidate did not pay one bill, even for cleaning his shoes.*"

In 1699 a petition from Chippenham was presented against one of the M. P's for corruption and bribery. Several witnesses thus testified on oath——

"I was promised two guineas if I would do my best to get a vote; I did my best, but I heard nothing of the two guineas."

"The agent suddenly offered to lend me fifty pounds. I did not want to borrow. He then promised me 20 bushels of wheat. I never got it."

"I was forbidden to fish in certain waters. Just before the election I was told I might fish where I pleased."

MEMBERS OF PARLIAMENT.

"A silver tobacco-box was given me with hopes I might find it useful."

"I am a shoemaker. I was told that they wanted a shoemaker very badly on their side, and the first shoemaker that offered should have no need to make any more shoes as long as he lived."

"An agent asked goody Seryl to sell her house. She demurred, when he sent out for some ale, and because it was not strong enough he mixed brandy with it; of which when the dame had partaken freely, he took the key of the house from her, and locked the door, and has kept possession ever since," *

Margaret Burgess said she got, down in hand, a nice dress for herself, and a waistcoat for her husband. Besides, if her husband would vote the right way, there was besides a bushel of wheat for her, and a pair of new breeches for " Master." " Master " said it was all true about the waistcoat, but he had'nt seen anything of the breeches."

After one election the following bill was presented by the landlord of the White Hart, then the principal Inn.

	£	s.	d.
Election Dinner	268	0	0
Beer and Porter . . .	18	11	0
21 doz. Cider at 18/- . . .	18	18	0
130 doz. Port Wine at 42/- .	273	0	0
24 doz. Lisbon at 42/- . .	58	0	0
15 doz. Sherry at 63/- . .	45	0	0
Brandy, Rum, &c. for Punch .	45	0	0

* Possession of a burgage house gave a vote, though occupied only for *one* day; another account says three days.

	£	s.	d.
Glass broke	2	16	0
China broke	1	10	0
Plates and dishes broke	3	5	0
Knives and forks lost	2	6	0
5 Door keepers meat and beer	3	8	0
Cooks, Waiters, &c.	15	18	0
Mr. Salway's bill	3	0	0
	£758	12	0

Four days after followed the Ball and Supper, and the landlord's bill, at about the same amount.

In 1741 Sir Robert Walpole had raised against his Ministry a powerful phalanx of noblemen and gentlemen, called the Country Party.

The Hanoverian and Jacobite factions then shook Great Britain from sea to sea, and every little village was convulsed with political strife. There was a contested election in Chippenham; the Government candidates (supporting Sir Robert Walpole), were Alexander Hume and John Frederick. Those of the Country Party were Sir Edmund Thomas and Edward Baynton Rolt. Anthony Guy, the oldest of the Burgesses of the town, was then High Sheriff, and exercised weighty influence; he supported the Government. The partisans of Thomas and Rolt conceived and executed a daring scheme for getting Guy out of the way. The Under-Sheriff, through illness, had neglected to make return of a writ, and under pretence of an attachment, they arrested the Sheriff himself, and kept him in custody at one of the Inns in Chippenham all night, though he offered £10,000 bail for his release. Next morning, at the instigation of John Norris, Adam Tuck of Langley Burrell, (who built and lived in the present Rectory House) and with the connivance of William Johnson, the Bailiff, they hurried him off to Devizes, where they held guard over him till the Chippenham election was over. The election was won by the Country Party by a majority of one vote only. On a petition against the return it was tried before a Committee of the whole House. The name of Chippenham now rang throughout the land. It was well known that on the issue of the Chippenham Petition depended the fate of a minister who had been in power fourteen years; and each party put forth its utmost strength. Walpole was defeated by 16 votes, and declared he would never sit in the house again.

About 1780, Mr. Dawkins, a wealthy West Indian Merchant, bought up burgage houses at ten times their value, and furious struggles followed which were carried on for twenty years,

"with the most rancourous feelings of party spirit, and party hatred; we have seen the most vindictive passions of the human mind raised and forced into action by election contests. How many did these contests send to an untimely end! How many men did they ruin in their religion and moral conduct, and in their commercial pursuits, while the town was declining in its markets and trade!"

That townsman of Chippenham, who thus commented on the sad condition of social life, continues to say in pathetic language——

"It was in this state of mental, moral, and political lowness that two events happened, which seemed finally to seal the doom of its sunken state, and to fix its irrevocable fate. The one, the failure of a townsman, whose pecuniary affairs were vast and extended, and who had taken a most active part in these contests;—the other event, one of much greater importance, that of the sale of the better half of the burgage houses to one owner."

"Thus"—exclaims the indignant patriot—

"Our poor degraded town, like a slave bound with a chain, was sold to the highest bidder."

"But"—he adds at last in a triumphant strain—

"The ills we feared and anticipated passed away in a most extraordinary manner; and the purchase of the borough was broken in pieces by the passing of the Great Reform Bill, which came like the Genius of Liberty to restore freedom to the captive, and burst his bonds asunder."

The names of M. P's for Chippenham from the Imperial Parliament of 1801 are as follows:—

1801—Fludyer
     Dawkins

1802—Dawkins
     Maitland

1806—Maitland
     Dawkins

1807—Maitland
     Dawkins

1812—Brooke
     Peel
       (*Afterwards Sir Robert*)

1818—Miles
     Blandford
       (*Marquis of*)

1820—Maddock
　　　Grosett

1826—Maitland
　　　Gye

1830—Neeld
　　　Pusey

1831—Neeld
　　　Boldero

[REFORMED PARLIAMENT.]

1833—Neeld
　　　Talbot

1835—Neeld
　　　Boldero

1841—Neeld
　　　Boldero

1847—Neeld
　　　Boldero

[REFORMED PARLIAMENT.]

1852—Neeld
　　　Boldero

1857—Boldero
　　　Nisbet

1859—Lysley
　　　Long

1865—Neeld
　　　Goldney

[The Reform Bill of 1866 left Chippenham but One Member.]

1868—Goldney

1874—Goldney

1880—Goldney

[The Reform Bill of 1880 annihilated Chippenham as a Borough, and threw the electors into the Division of North-West Wilts.]

THE BAILIFFS.

The names of some of the early Bailiffs have been recorded in a former chapter.

Lord Hungerford held the office in the reign of Henry VIII, and on his attainder the King granted the Bailiwick to two of his courtiers, Robert Searle and Laurence Walmesley.

The first Bailiff (as recited) under Queen Mary's Charter, Henry Farnewell (*alias* Goldney), and the first twelve Burgesses, were nominated by the Queen herself. Immediately after their election they proceeded " *with the consent of the Chief Commons* " *to make Ordinances and Decrees*

" for euer more to be deulye observed and thoroughlye kepte to the advancem^t of the glorye of God & the utilitye & ornam^t of the publique weal."

——If a Bailiff refuse to deliver his accounts, he shall be fined £40——If an inhabitant refuse to assist the Bailiff in maintaining order, he shall lose his freedom. ——If any person shall dissever himself from the politic head, he shall exercise no trade in the borough, and be fined or imprisoned.——No person shall admit "foreyners," or receive apprentices, without leave of the Bailiff. ——Every householder shall help to repair the Butts at the Ivy, and in St. Mary's Street.——Any baker selling false weight of bread shall for the first offence be fined 3s. 4d.; for the second 6s. 8d.; for the third "*subibit judicium Pilloræ*" (shall be punished in the pillory), and no "foreyne" bread shall be sold.——No Tipler (retail dealer) shall set up "tipling" without license; ale shall be sold at a penny a gallon; and shall be examined by the ale taster.——Every inhabitant shall have in his house a club, and shall come forth with the same when need shall require; and all persons drawing a weapon to strike a townsman, or who shall call him by an opprobrious name, shall be punished in the open stocks.——Any butcher, baker, brewer, poulterer, cook, costermonger, or fruiterer, who shall conspire not to sell victuals but at certain prices, shall forfeit £10, or suffer imprisonment twenty days on bread and water.——Every householder shall from May 1st to Sep. 8th set at his door a barrel or pail continually full of water (in case of fire, the houses being built of wood and thatched, and iron crooks were provided for pulling off the thatch). ——If any burgess behave contemptuously to the Bailiff, or call him knave, or such like, he shall be debarred all benefit of the borough lands.*——Searchers of leather shall be appointed to make a trial of shoes, and to see that all manner of leather be sufficiently tanned, wrought, and dyed.†——No man without special license shall kill, or sell, or dress, or eat any flesh in the time of Lent.‡——No inhabitant shall divide his tenement into diverse portions.——

The Bailiff was sworn to bear true allegiance to the Sovereign, to keep peace, and minister justice, sparing none for favour; to observe the assize of bread;

* Householders were again and again disfranchized and debarred on being convicted "*for opprobrious words spoken against the Bailiff and fraternity by calling them Knaves, and other scurrilous language.*"

† 26 Oct, 1605, nine pairs of shoes were seized in the open Fair by the Searchers, which say on oath "*that the said shoes are made part of calf's leather; wherefore all are forfeited according to the Statute.*"

‡ An Act of Parliament was passed A.D. 1569, to encourage the Fisheries, requiring that every Wednesday and Saturday in Lent should be kept as Fish Days, and no manner of flesh be eaten, and the penalty of disobedience was £3 for each offence; but sick and weakly persons might obtain a dispensation. The Jury impanelled to enforce the law say—" 1606—Ap. 14—*Thomas and Robert Baker, butchers, have sold flesh this Lent, and this morning offered for sale in their shop veal and mutton.*"

to maintain the liberties of the Borough, keep true accounts; and "*all other things which appertain to your office you shall well and faithfullye execute, so neere as God shall give you grace.*"

A Burgess or freeman was charged——"*You shall a faithful and true Burgess be to this Boroughe, willinglye obey and assiste your Bayliffe, not disclose his secrets, mayntayne all lawful franchises* and behave yourself as a faithful member to the uttermoste of your power——So helpe you God in his promise conteyned in His most holye Worde.*"

The list of Bailiffs and Mayors is perfect, (with the exception of thirteen unrecorded names), from 1554 to 1893; they are three hundred and fifty one in number. One Bailiff was a clergyman, the Revd. Richard Weaver, in 1800.

After an Election in 1661, the Bailiff made a double return of Members, Edward Hungerford and Henry Baynton, and Hugh Speke and Francis Gwyn. The House of Commons voted that the election was void "*by sinful miscarriage of the Bailiff herein; and that the Speaker be desired to issue his warrant to the Clerk of the Crown that he do send the Serjeant-at-Arms to take the Bailiff into custody, and bring him up to answer his insolent carriage before the Committee.*"

OUTRAGEOUS HOSE. It is almost beyond belief to what absurd extravagancies of dress gentlemen went in

---

* There were High Burgesses, and Petit Burgesses called the Commons——these last possessed some powers apart from the Corporation.

the days of Queen Elizabeth. They wore TRUNK HOSE or short breeches, stuffed with horsehair like wool sacks; the outer materials were silk taffeta, or other rich stuff, worked in gold and silver thread, laced and slashed, and pinked, and pointed; and to such ridiculous excess had the fashion run, that the Virgin Queen, early in her reign, launched her Proclamation to restrain the exuberant enlargement of gentlemen's costume.

All tailors were bound over by the Magistrates to obey the law under a penalty of £20; the bonds of the seven tailors of Chippenham in the Borough chest show that they entered into the due recognizances.

"The Quenes Maj^{tie} by Her Highness proclamacon for Reformacon of the monstruous & outragious greatness of hosen forbyds all Taylors w^{tin} her Realmes to make any hosen of the sayd outragious greatnes & y^t no taylour put into the outside of any pair of hosen but 1¼ yard of stuffe, and in compass but 1 yard and ½qr for the tallest person, and for persons of less stature to put lesse, and to put no more lyninge but one lyning of linen and one other lyning of stuffe wrought within Her Highnes domynyons, May 6, 1566."

Feb. 27, 1756, the following statute condemned a cruel, but ancient amusement.

"The Custom of Throwing at Cocks on Shrove Tuesdays being in itself a most barbarous Practice and not only inconsistent with the laws both of God and man, but greatly tends to the training up of youth in principles of inhumanity, and must give offence to every good Christian who considers the animal world was made for his use and not abuse we order that no person within this Borough shall Throw, Pelt, Squail or Shoot at any Cock, Hen, Pullet, or Chick, or any Feathered Fowl of any kind while living, under a penalty of 20s."

THE PILLORY. The Pillory stood near the gates of the Churchyard; probably close to it was

THE WHIPPING POST, as there is an entry among the Church accounts of A.D. 1677—

For the post, and work done at the Church hatch . 8d.

In the Borough books are these memoranda of expenses* incurred in the endeavour to improve public behaviour——

		s.	d.
A.D. 1598. For canvas iiij ells to make a good shirt, and whip		4	0
,, For whipping rogues and making a shirt		0	4
,, 1676. For the whipping post and pillory		15	0

It were well if the unsparing use of the "whip and the shirt" were revived in these days, as the most effective and wholesome punishment of brutal and cowardly ruffians, especially those guilty of criminal assaults on children. The "cat o' nine tails" is the only executive these scoundrels fear; and it ought to be administered with the extremest severity that the body can endure during a long period of penal imprisonment.

* It seems that the Church and Town divided the cost of the repairs of the Pillory, for we read in a Churchwarden's Book (1667)

	£	s.	d.
Paid for stone and work at the pillory	1	2	6
,, lead at the pillory		1	6
,, hauling stone from Hazlebury for the pillory		4	0
,, iron used about the pillory			4

It is likely that another ancient instrumentality for the correction of the rogues of the Borough, often mentioned by the name of "THE STOCKS," was not far from the "corner of terrors," where stood the Pillory and Whipping Post. The Borough Gaol, or Blind House, was under the Town Hall; it was of service not only as the prison for the delinquents of the town, but for other classes of malefactors—we read of "*six piratts in custody,*" here.

In 1784 The BOROUGH LANDS were measured and mapped, and found to contain 141½ acres—so that 75 acres had been sold or lost since the Charter was granted; and no Minutes in the books of the Borough evidence how or when they passed out of the hands of the Corporation. But from documents among vast heaps of Hungerford MSS, it is pretty certain that young Lord Hungerford after he succeeded to the inheritance of his fathers in 1555, made strenuous endeavours to regain also that part of Chippenham Hundred which had been alienated by Queen Mary; and though the Corporation resisted the aggression, and (as it appears) won an early suit, yet, as the wealth and influence of all the Hungerfords, then the most potent family in the County, were arrayed against them, it is likely they made early peace with their mighty neighbour across the river, and by sale or compromise, (or from legal compulsion) surrendered to him his patrimonial property of Rowden Down and the coppices. Certain it is that in A.D. 1603, a Hungerford was a Chippenham M.P.; so in 1620: and Sir Edward Hungerford represented the Borough through all the years of the Commonwealth to A.D. 1680.

In 1604 (and often afterwards) the Town propitiated their Members and friends by the present of a Sugar-Loaf, weighing 10 lbs. at 2/- a lb, equal in our money to 8/-* Sir Francis Popham, M.P., a generous benefactor to Chippenham, often received presents of Sugar, with pottles of Sack, and a Horse that cost £12. Bishop Burnet was complimented with a gift of sugar and wine while he sojourned in the town in 1689.

THE TOWN

About the middle of 1700 or a little earlier, the London Road was brought through the town, parallel to the Causeway; before that time the London coaches drove by the White Hart Inn along St. Mary's Street.

A.D. 1784, a Borough and Town Map, on a large scale, was drawn by John Powell, land surveyor. The STREETS at that time were——

High Street	Lord's Lane
Market Place	Causeway
Middle Street	Joseph's Lane
New Lane	St. Mary's Street
Timber Street	Cook Street

* Tea was then sold at £1 a lb., equal to £4.

Blind Lane
Back Lane
West Mead Lane
Wood Lane
Barley Close Lane
King Street

The Butts
Embery Lane
Baidon's Lane
Winnick's Lane
Land's End Lane
Rotten Row

The TAVERNS were
The Old Bell
„ Pack Horse
„ Three Crowns
„ Coopers' Arms
„ Nap
„ Lamb
„ Rose and Crown
„ Bear
„ Angel
„ George
„ Anchor
" Little George

The Horse and Jockey
„ White Hart (2)
„ Cock
„ White Lion
„ Hat and Feathers
„ New
„ Swan
„ Seven Stars
„ Gun
„ Duke William
„ King's Head
„ Black Horse (2)

In other days there were The Bell—The Holy Lamb —The Red Lion—The Antelope—The Bull—The Shears.

HOUSES. In a house at the corner of Wood Lane, in a window on the landing were several quarries of stained glass, with a sickle, and raven chained and collared—devices of the Hungerfords.

The architectural elevations of the Old White Hart, and the extent of its façade, with its fine bays and oriel windows suggest that it was once the mansion of the Lord of the Hundred.

A house in the High Street presents a richly ornamental frontage in a pure, Corinthian style of architecture: this fine façade formed the central elevation of a large house on Bowden Hill, the external walls of which only were built. It was removed to Chippenham about 150 years ago. It is said to have been designed by Inigo Jones, or one of his pupils.

The gabled roofs and dormer windows of many of the houses in the town carry back the date of their erection to the reign of Queen Elizabeth, and earlier.

"*There was about 20 years ago an old house standing close to the Angel Inn, which, from time immemorial, had been denominated* THE PALACE, *and was supposed to have constituted a part of the residence bequeathed by Alfred to his daughter; but its massive walls, and heavy pointed arch indicated a much later construction than the Saxon period. We conjecture therefore that it was built in Norman times on the site which the Palace occupied.*"

JOHN BRITTON—1814.

Sheldon Manor House stands on the side of a hill commanding an extensive view towards Chippenham. It was built by the Gascelyns, lords of the Manor cir. A.D. 1300. The porch is lofty and massive, supported by heavy, handsome buttresses; the roof is formed of solid intersecting arches of stone, serving to support the stone floor of the domestic chapel above, which has a fine timbered roof. This noble porch belonged to a much larger mansion than the present Farm-House, which dates only from the time of Elizabeth, and was built by the Hungerfords.

Eastward of the House is the Chapel of the estate, desecrated, but little injured in fabric. The east arch is traceable, and in the north and south walls are two Decorated windows, very gems of beauty, cinquefoiled, with the cusps of the arcs still sharp and perfect.

At a moderate cost this Chapel might be recovered, and re-dedicated to God, so as to supply a Service, (if not on Sundays, at least on some week-day), for the use of the near farms, and for the cottages in the scattered hamlet of Sheldon.

Aubrey refers to Fowlswick as "*an ancient howse with a fair mote about*"——the date of 1679 on the present house shows that it was built *temp.* Charles II.: a huge fire place, 10 feet wide, surmounted by a ponderous chimney, speaks of a former mansion of great size and strength. It was protected by a wide deep moat, (still remaining), which enclosed a homestead of three acres. Many coins have been found here.

The present Vicarage House of Chippenham was some time the residence of the Rogers Family. Their arms, 3 *stags*, are cut on a stone-shield inserted in the south wall of the garden. The house passed from the Rogers to the Hollands.

Rogers Holland, who lived there many years, was M.P. for Chippenham from 1727 to 1741, when he was appointed Judge of the counties of Carnarvon, Merioneth, and Anglesey. About 1802 it was occupied by Mrs. Hungerford, the widow of the last of that family. In 1826 it was conveyed to the benefice in exchange for the old Vicarage House now standing on the south of the Churchyard.

THE TOWN PUMP. An antiquated building stood over a large ancient well in the rising ground on the highest part of the Market Place, immemorially known as the Town Pump, which bore on the pediment the arms of Sir Edward Hungerford, and on the roundel this inscription——

"ERECTED BY SIR EDWARD HUNGERFORD, 1679."

For many generations this Well was the only source within the Borough from which the inhabitants obtained water; but as the population increased, and other wells were dug, it was neglected, and fell into ruin. It belonged, (as sunk in the waste of the Market Place), to the lord of the Manor. In 1766, it was held from William Norris, M.P. of Nonsuch House, Bromham, on lease, by T. Eacott, but was then closed and useless. In 1768, in consideration of £16 10s. paid to Eacott for the surrender of his lease, and of an annual rent of 7s. 6d. to the lord of the Manor, the Well, and the ground around it, were assigned to the Town. A space was railed in, and a new, strong pump was made, but it could be used only by those who paid for the water—— except in case of fire, when water was free.

It had often been proposed to bring the waters of Lockswell Spring into Chippenham; it was affirmed that it would furnish a daily supply of 100,000 gallons of most salubrious water; as its source was at the top of a hill in Nethermore, 120 feet higher than Chippenham, no mechanical pressure would be necessary, but by natural gravitating power it would flow over all the town, and could throw a *jet d'eau* from a fountain in the Market Place as high as the spire of the Parish Church.

THE TOWN WELL. Owing to the circumstance that Chippenham had been for years visited by typhoid fever and other dangerous epidemics which at last settled upon the town and could not be dislodged, and caused many lamentable deaths, it was suspected that the water of the wells was not pure, and on test of many it became evident that they were to an alarming degree contaminated with sewage, which found no difficulty in percolating the porous rock on which Chippenham lay.

In 1872 water was taken from the Avon above its junction with the Marden—from the Marden—from the Foundry Well—and from Lockswell Spring, and a sample of each was subjected to severe examination by eminent analysts. The tests applied revealed these facts——that the waters of the two rivers were identical in character, and contained so much deposit of organic matter that they would be dangerous for drinking, unless they were filtrated with scientific care over deep beds of gravel——that the water of the Foundry Well was hard, but in all other respects good and wholesome——but that of all the waters submitted to analysis those of Lockswell were unquestionably the best, perfectly pure and wholesome, clear and soft, and fit for every domestic use——there was therefore no doubt whatever about the selection of the Lockswell water for Chippenham.

This water is not given out (as was supposed) by the Lower Greensand, but by the Lower Calcareous Grit, an arenaceous deposit of variable thickness, forming the base of the Coralline Oolite, and running along between the Coral Rag and Oxford Clay, on which it rests. The Calcareous Grit serves as a storage for water, but as a rule gives out only small springs—the Oxford Clay is stiff and impermeable and rests on Sandstones, representing Kellaways Rock, which is no worthy reservoir of water.

Lockswell Spring was carefully gauged in 1873, and found then to flow at the rate of 46 gallons a minute, that is, it rendered 66,240 gals. a day: but it was understood that in very dry weather the quantity to be depended on would not exceed 50,000 gals. a day.

This would not be nearly sufficient for the population of Chippenham; nor would the smaller springs in Nethermore and Bowden Hill, united with Lockswell, be of any appreciable service.

The population of Chippenham in 1871 was 5202. The Government required 15 gallons of water a day for every inhabitant, including infants. Therefore the daily supply of water for the town of Chippenham must exceed 78,000 gals.——and provision ought to be made for a probable increase in the population.

Thus all hope of making use of the Lockswell water ——the merits of which the monks of Stanley knew so well and valued so much that, 650 years ago, they had it conveyed to their Abbey, a distance of three miles—— that spring upon which a few far-seeing, thinking men of Chippenham had looked for generations with a longing eye as the special gift of GOD for the health of their native town, and which the Corporation of Chippenham ought to have secured centuries ago at any cost——was necessarily and absolutely abandoned.

The Corporation (1873) wisely determined to sink a well on their own land. Upon the advice of an eminent geologist a site was chosen in West Mead. A shaft was sunk. It passed through the strata predicted. Water was found in the Greater Oolite, and in abundant volume. This water is a little hard, (as the shaft did not reach the Fuller's Earth, which supplies the softest water), but it is of excellent quality, pure, clear, well aerated, and flows from a deep and constant source, not subject to local influences.

THE CROSS. The Market Cross of Chippenham, (probably of the same character and proportions as those handsome ecclesiastical memorials yet existing at Malmesbury and Castle Combe) which by its silent teaching warned the buyers and sellers to remember GOD in the Market, is thus referred to in the Borough Minutes——

—"A.D. 1658——for mending the Crosse, and 2 sacks of lyme for the Crosse."

It is mentioned also in an indenture by Sir Ed. Hungerford, who leases—

—"A.D. 1683——a parcel of grounde on the north east side of the Butter Crosse in Chippenham, and near the sayd Butter Crosse—"

"*Here*" (John Aubrey says of Kington Cross), "*in those days was a market for fish, eggs, butter, and such small gear.*"

TRADE.

CORN. Lying at the foot of the Chalk downs, which produce fine crops of wheat and barley, Chippenham was once famous for its large Corn Market. The colliers from the Somerset mines used to bring up coal in sacks on packhorses and mules, and load back with corn and cloth. This was almost the only mode of conveyance, and the number of these beasts of burden was amazingly large. The dealers from Bristol carried on an active trade with Chippenham in wheat and oats and barley, until the farmers began to take samples of their corn to Bristol Market in bags——whence they were nick-named "*Baggers*," or more commonly "*Badgers*," and the western dealers in a great degree forsook Chippenham. The contentions between the Wiltshire Corn Merchants and the Bristol "Badgers" gave the Justices of Petty Sessions and the Bailiffs of Chippenham much trouble. Notices of these unwelcome visitors often occur——

"A.D. 1622——For stayeing Badgers and keeping a note of their names."

"For restraining Badgers coming to the Marketts here to engrosse corn."

King George III. while in Wilts, heard of these factors, and said—"*Bad! Bad! Bad!—down the Severn come the Badgers, and spoil the markets.*"

CLOTH. Woollen Cloths, Kerseymeres, blankets, &c. formed for a long period a staple manufacture in Chippenham. From the reign of Elizabeth to the close of the 18th century, the towns in the valley of the Avon—Malmesbury, Chippenham, Trowbridge, and Bradford, with all the circumjacent villages, were largely employed in weaving woollen fabrics, and the master-clothiers became men of wealth and dignity.

In 1790 there were about sixty Cloth Factories in Chippenham, all busy and prosperous. They were not *Factories* in the present sense of the word, but rather Cloth Shops, in which the finishing processes were effected——the spinning, carding, warping, and weaving being carried on by families in almost every cottage in the town and country.*

This manufacture declined very rapidly in Wiltshire owing to the introduction of the Power Loom in the great factories of Yorkshire and Lancashire, and large consignments of cloth were returned upon the makers' hands. The clothiers of Chippenham received their death-blow in consequence of the riots, which continued through 1801-2-3, and became very alarming; neither

---

* There is a reference to Chippenham and its Clothiers in Churchill's Poems—THE GHOST; Book III—
    Banished to Chippenham or Frome
    Dullman once more shall ply the loom;
    Crape, lifting up his hands and eyes,
    " Dullman—the loom at Chippenham!"—cries.

property nor life was safe. In 1838 the weavers were in great distress: out of 86 men who depended on the trade for their livelihood, only 31 were at work, and their earnings were only on an average 8s. 2½d. a week.

TOKENS. Tokens were used by nearly every tradesman as advertisements, but were only payable at the shop whence they were issued. Some were Penny, some Halfpenny, some Farthing Tokens. Of Chippenham Tokens nine are in the Museum at Devizes, and are all of the third value.

1. *Obverse* WILL . ADYE. Mercer
   Reverse In Chippenham. 1665.
2. „ „ JOHN . EDWARDS.
   Of Chippenham. 1665. Linen Draper
3. „ „ SAMVELL . ELLIOTE. Two swords crossed
   and a Carbine
   Of Chippenham. 1666.
4. „ „ SAMVELL . GAGE. of. Tallow Chandlers'
   Arms
   Chippenham. 1653.
5. „ „ JOHN . HEORMAN. A Wool Comb
   In Chippenham. 1671.
6. „ „ HENRY . LAMBERT. In. Mercers' Arms
   Chippenham. Mercer.
7. „ „ BRISTOW . PLACE.
   Chippenham. 1665.
8. „ „ JOHN . SHORTE. Chandlers' Arms
   In Chippenham.
9. „ „ JOHN . STEVENS. Of.
   Chippenham. 1632.

VIEW OF CHIPPENHAM.
From an Original Drawing by John Britton, F.S.A. A.D. 1810.

Two other tokens, not at Devizes, are: John A. Willsheare and Andrew Wilcox, 1688.

These semi-legal coins were current only between 1650 and 1672, when copper money was very scarce in England. When the farthing of Charles II. was ready to issue from the Mint all tokens were driven out of circulation by stringent proclamation. They continued, however, to pass with authorised copper coins till the present bronze coinage was issued.

THE BRIDGE.

Of Chippenham Bridge John Britton thus writes—

"This Bridge is traditionally reported to have been the gift of Queen Elizabeth, who visited Chippenham during one of her progresses through England"——

He admits that the tradition is falsified by her sister's Charter (four years before), which provided means for the "*reparations of a certain great bridge built over the River of Avon.*" Nevertheless, it is not improbable that Elizabeth* supplemented her sister's bounty.

---

* When this Queen was in Bristol and saw the dirty garments of the women, she said—" *Oddsbodikins!—these Bristol women shall have a drying ground!*"; and the Bristol women hold the drying ground to this day. When Her Highness, with her heavy and haughty retinue, was riding over the trembling arches of Chippenham Bridge, in danger every minute of being precipitated into the "water of Avon," and crushed by falling stones, it is in accordance with her habit to have said, "*Oddsbodikins!—these Chippenham people shall have a new bridge,*"—and to have remitted to the Bailiff a generous donation from her Exchequer. But the gift is not recorded.

"In A.D. 1578, it is mentioned as a "*greate stoned bridge conteyning xv arches;*" it was twenty feet wide, but seems to have been so weak and shattered, that it was not considered safe even for packhorses. Wheeled vehicles never used it; and the heavy coaches and waggons from Bath to London turned down Foghamshire Lane, went up Monkton Hill through Cocklebury, and crossed the river either at the Old or the New Ford. In 1605 the Bridge was in great decay; in 1615 two arches and piers fell into the water; and as the cost of repairs amounted to nearly £100, and as a rate laid on all the inhabitants could

——"verye hardlye be brought to passe and of some never to be hoped for by reason of their inhabillitye and weeke estate, many not getting mainteynance for this present lief——"
the cost was raised upon the Borough lands.

So frail and crazy was the aged structure that in the severe winter of 1685 it was feared it would be carried away by the floods, and men were set "*to help the great pieces of Ice through the Arches of the Bridge in the great ffroste.*"

It was repeatedly under repair throughout the eighteenth century, was strengthened and widened and lengthened from time to time at great cost, till in 1796 "*according to a plan made by the Rev. Mr. Weaver,*" (afterwards Bailiff) it underwent a substantial restoration and expansion—it was widened 30 feet—more arches were added—the piers were laid on massive bases—and a symmetrical balustrade and parapet were added.

———" The Bridge is a very handsome structure, and strikes every stranger as being a great ornament to the Town; the fine sweep on the Bath road deserves very high commendation; and when we consider its being built at the expense of the Corporation, and not of the County, we must allow it to reflect credit on the spirit and age when the improvement was made."

To meet the heavy charge of these alterations and extensions the landed property of the Town was mortgaged to the amount of £1200, and the Burgesses considerately agreed that

———" no more treats be given on the election of Bailiff, being attended with very large expense."

THE CAUSEWAY.

Queen Mary granted her Charter

    I. For the better government and rule of the Borough.

   II. For the maintenance of Two Burgesses at Parliament.

  III. For the reparations of a certain great Bridge over the River of Avon.

  IV. For the reparations of a certain bank or way called a "Cawsaye."

"*From the tyme whereof noe man knowes to the contrary there was and is a certaine cawsey leading from the markett towne of Chippenham towards the markett towne of*

Calne for all the King's subjects as well footmen as horsemen to goe and ride which conteyneth in length 2 miles & in breadth 10 *foot lying in the parish of Chippenham."*

This Causeway must have been constructed in the earliest days of Chippenham's existence. The low flat country toward Derry Hill was in ancient times so swampy as to be impassable. The little stream called the Pewe, was frequently flooding the pathway, and there were continual complaints against the Abbot of of Stanley (to whom Pewsham Forest belonged) that he did not keep his brook within its limits. The Causeway, therefore, was made, of necessity, centuries before it is referred to in the Charter.

It was cut through the Forest, and was raised so high above flooded levels, that it is called " a bank ;" and was pitched with stone so as to serve for packhorses as well as for foot passengers; for this reason the pitching was carried to the top of Derry Hill.

Long after Mary's days it was the only highway from Chippenham into the heart of Wilts, and it seems never to have been well constructed, as ever needing heavy repairs. And indeed its reparation was an expensive work, if it cost as much as Maud Heath's Causeway on the north, *viz.* £400 a mile. No wonder the Queen speaks feelingly of the inhabitants of Chippenham being "*grieviously burthened & driven & compelled to bestow great costs*" on their Bridge and Causeway. Until she provided funds, though very scanty, for keeping the Causeway in order, only the voluntary offerings of travellers, received by the Hermit, were chiefly available for that purpose.

"1604. In making a trench near the Hermitage by the Causey for the preservation thereof." *Borough Records.*

The existence and position of the Hermitage are well assured by tradition. It stood on the right side of the Causeway, nearly opposite the Pack Horse, on the London Road, about half a mile from the town.* The Hermit was licensed by the Bishop, and allowed to celebrate certain religious offices for travellers in the little chapel which adjoined his dwelling—he professed before GOD that he would be obedient to the Church; would lead a sober and chaste life, avoid taverns, and say continual prayers;—

"And the goods that I may get by free gift of Christian people, or by bequest,† or testament, (reserving only necessaries to my sustenance) I shall truly without deceit lay out upon reparation and amending the Common Way belonging to the town."

After 1554 the Causeway became legally chargeable upon the Borough. ‡

---

* In the Protector Somerset's Register of the Wilts Estates (MS. at Longleat) under "Monkton in Chippenham," which belonged to him, it is noted——

——' Tharmyte (*i.e.* the Hermit) holdyth without copye iij acres of pasture lying in ij paroks (*i.e.* paddocks, still called the Causeway Pieces) by th' army-tage.'

† Hermits were often endowed, as he of Codford, on whom Oliver de Ingham devised two acres of land.

‡ 1634. The Hermit's cell seems to have been occupied as a cottage, as amongst the Baptisms is recorded——' Margaret, daughter of Wm. Jones, Hermitage.'

But as late as 1685, an Information was laid that——

——" the cawsey was and is in great decay soe that the King's Subjects cannot passe and repasse over the same without perill of their lives and losse of their goods to the great Damage of the King's subjects."

In the course of years when vehicles began to force a passage through the Forest parallel with the Causeway, it was found necessary to guard the Causeway with sarsen stones from the trespass of wheels.

THE PLAGUE.

In 1608, and in the three following years, the Plague raged among the population of England. At Chippenham, fairs and markets were closed, because in certain towns adjoining, as Calne and Corsham, the pestilence had broken out; and special constables were appointed *" to watch and warde suspected visitors,"* and on one occasion

——" to Keepe one Nicholas Eaton & his Wief out of the Towne upon the speach given forth that they had bene amonge infected psons."

Notwithstanding all precautions the mortal malady invaded Chippenham at Whitsuntide, 1611, and *"for 5 months remayned in the borough in most fearful manner"*; many fled; many died;* the magistrates authorised collections from the country round, and the infected sick

---

* " 1611—181 were buried this year, whereof 130 were of the plague." *Church Register.*

and distressed were relieved *" in verye Christian sorte and commisaret manner—Thankes be given unto* GOD *for all his mercyes—"*

In 1636, London and other towns were again visited by the Plague, and on the discovery that some of the inhabitants of Chippenham were

———" verye negligent in enterteyninge in theire Houses all sorts of psns (as well of the said Citye of London as elsewhere) Wherebye the said Borough hath bin and is greatelye endaungered to bee infected with the saide Disease —— Did not the LORDE in mercye prserve the same ——"

it was ordered that no person

———" Shall enterteyne anyo Straunger or Straungers whatsoever, untill it shall please GOD to withdraw from among us the said Disease."

Hardly to be less dreaded than the Asiatic Plague was that loathsome and desolating sickness, the Small Pox. It fell heavily on Chippenham in the summer of 1711. In a Sermon* preached by Thomas Frampton, M.A. (not Vicar of Chippenham, but resident in the town during the year, and afterwards Vicar of Shrewton,) on Sunday, Nov. 18, after the sickness had abated, he alludes to the misery and suffering through which they had passed.

His text was—"WHAT REWARD SHALL I GIVE

---

* PIETY and CHARITY, the best Return for Mercies Explained in a Sermon preached in the Parish Church of Chippenham. Nov. 18, 1711.
Bristol: Printed and Sold by W. Bonny, and R. Warne, in Chippenham, 1712.

UNTO THE LORD FOR ALL THE BENEFITS THAT HE HATH DONE UNTO ME?" Psalm 116. 11 v.——

"My design is to put you of this Place in Mind of the Blessings you have received in Relation to the Distemper that lately reign'd among us, and from which we are in a great Measure deliver'd.

In the time of the late Sickness the last thing we usually heard at Night was a Funeral Knell, and the First Thing that was commonly told us in the Morning was the Death of some Neighbour or Friend. We could barely walk the streets without being a Terrour to our neighbours, nor could many of our neighbours do the same without being a Terrour to us. The country about us would neither store our Markets, nor frequent our Shops. A numerous poor lay hard upon us, whom we could hardly relieve without injuring our Families; nor neglect without injuring the Faith.

Now to our comfort 'tis much otherwise. And what makes the Blessing the more Remarkable is, that our Affliction was remov'd so soon: In one summer the Visitation began, and for the most part ended with us. If it had continu'd much longer, how heavy and afflicting had it been to us."

He reminds his audience of the tormenting pains, sad frights, and amazing agonies that overwhelmed them under the distemper, how often they lost their sight and senses, how their best friends fled to hide themselves—and now they are safely restored to their Church, their houses, and families. They must impute the mercy received not to their own foresight, or skill, or constitution, but to the goodness of GOD alone.

―――"And here"―he continues―"I cannot but adore the infinite Goodness of GOD, who expects nothing from us for all his Benefits, but the doing that which intitles us to his Favour. He makes his Goodness to us a Motive to our Piety, that from our Piety he may take Occasion to renew his Goodness."―――

In token of their gratitude, and as "an Act of Piety to GOD," the Preacher suggests:—I. A better observance of the LORD's Day by all the parishioners of Chippenham—"*this would be a Noble Act of Piety, and would look as if the Parish were truly sensible of the Blessing received.*"—II. As the "Keeping of GOD's Sabbath" is not more dear to Him than the "reverence of His Sanctuary," he recommends they should restore the Church, and make the House of Prayer the "Beauty of Holiness,"—"*this likewise would be looked upon as a Brave Act of Piety.*"—III. It seems that the Music and Singing in Church were but inefficiently rendered; he asks whether it is not reasonable to sing Psalms upon the account of mercies received, and to promote such Harmony that their Piety may make their Praise one of the "Sweet Songs of Zion."—IV. The Preacher next speaks nervously, as he feels he is treading on tender ground, when he says——

"GOD's House, or Day, is not more Dear to Him than His Servants; but here we Ministers can say but little, because it would look as if we preached up Ourselves, and yet somewhat ought to be said, because if We don't *magnifie our Office*, I know not who will. If therefore some publick Acknowledgment was paid to your Minister as a pious Requital to him for his Prayers and Pains, and in him to GOD for His Mercy and Goodness, I question not but it would be accounted a *Sweet smelling Sacrifice to the* LORD."——

——V. He advises that as the Parishioners should sanctify their souls by constant attendance at Church, so should they sanctify their houses with Family Prayer, humble adoration, and holy praise; and redouble their joy and love,—"*and as you have tasted how good* GOD *is, sin no more lest a worse thing happen to you.*"——VI. He bids the public authorities amend some practices of public injustice. There was a loud complaint that the poor of the town were defrauded—and such complaints do pierce the ear of GOD, and it might be that the Small Pox was a judgment from Him—and the reason why corn was not now brought to Chippenham Market (as in former days) might be that the market was forestalled and the poor were robbed in price, weight, and measure. He also urges upon private persons, especially those whom GOD had saved in their distress, to shew mercies to the suffering poor, and lessen their miseries.—— VII. As there was no provision in the town for the general education of the children, he thinks it would be a further proof of their gratitude if they would immediately establish Free Charity Schools—and then concludes in the following caustic words—

——"FOR YOUR INTEREST YOU OUGHT TO SUPPORT

THIS DESIGN, AND LET ME ADD FOR YOUR CREDIT. ILL THINGS HAVE BEEN SPOKEN OF YOU. I WISH BY SUCH GOOD ACTIONS YOU'D SHEW THAT YOU DESERVE IT NOT."

Mr. Frampton's recommendation fell on unsympathetic ears: for, with the sole exception of a bequest of the Vicar,* no effort was made to found a National School until 1824: and when Mr. Short, the Vicar, applied to the Corporation for a subscription, they unanimously declined.

THE SCHOOL.

Richard Scott, by his will, dated 28th May, 1661, directed that——

——" Whensoever a School shall be erected and maintained, my house in Cooke's Street shall be given for the further encouragement of the Schoolmaster, and be applied to that use by the Bailiff and Burgesses for ever."

William Woodruffe, of Chippenham, gave by will, (1664) to the Bailiff of the town, and to the Minister of the Church, an annuity of £5 to be paid to a Schoolmaster for teaching Ten poor boys: this sum to be paid out of the Ivy property on the production of a certi-

---

* Robert Cock, Vicar of Chippenham at this time (from 1704 to 1716) left by will £50 *(which was all that he had)* for teaching poor girls to read, and instructing them in the knowledge and practice of the Christian religion. A field of 2 ac. 3 roo. at Hardenhuish was purchased with this legacy, the rent of which is still applied as the donor wished.

ficate from the Vicar and Bailiff that the boys are duly educated.

Upon the payment of this bequest the house given by Richard Scott was occupied and used as a Free School. It was kept in repair by the Corporation, and the Master paid no rent. It consisted of a large school-room, and five other rooms; there was no garden.* But it appears the premises had not yet been legally transferred, and in the course of sixty years had become ruinous.

By indenture, dated 27th of Decr. 1733, between Richard Scott (great grandson of the above) and the Bailiff and Burgesses of the Borough, it was recited that a School had been erected and maintenance given. Therefore Richard Scott, the younger, *for confirming the charitable benevolence of his ancestor*, conveyed to the Bailiff and Burgesses, and their successors for ever, the decayed tenement in Cooke Street, with the plot of ground on which it stood, that the premises and rents might be applied according to his great-grand-father's will; and gave also himself £20 for the repairs of the house.

Ten Pounds were left by Mrs. Mary Bridges, of Chippenham, for the use of the Free School, in 1764, which, with interest of £5, were paid to the Bailiff, who engaged, for himself and successors, to pay 15 shillings a year to the Master of the School for teaching two poor boys on the Bailiff's nomination. The twelve Free boys paid 1s. a year each for fires, pens, and ink.

---

* "The School fell into abeyance for a time, and was opened again in April, 1713, for 24 boys, with a benefaction of £10 per ann. in land." *Present State of Charity Schools*, 1713.

THE FIRE OF LONDON.

There is a serious suspicion that the Great Fire of London, in 1666, was the issue of a malign conspiracy.——And it has been confidently asserted that the horrific plot itself was actually hatched in the streets of Chippenham!

A short time after the dread Conflagration, a Committee of the House of Commons was appointed to "*sit and enquire into the circumstances of the Firing of the City of London.*" Before this Commission appeared William Duckett, Esqr. of Hartham, M.P. and deposed*——

That one Harry Baker, of Chippenham, County of Wilts, coming from Chippenham Market on the Thursday before the Fire began in London, met one John Woodman, of Kelloways, in the same county, and had some discourse about a yoke of fat bullocks which Woodman wished to sell, and which Baker was willing to buy, if Woodman would keep them a little longer on his hands. This Woodman declined to do, for that he could not stay any longer in the county; and on Baker asking him whither he was going, he refused to tell him, and said, "*What hast thee to do to make that question?*" But riding a little further, the said

---

* Report of Sir Robert Brook, Chairman of the Committee appointed by the House of Commons to enquire into the Firing of the City of London, made 22 Jan. 1667.

Woodman expressed himself to Henry Baker in these words——

"You are brave blades at Chippenham—you made bonfires lately for beating the Dutch—but since you delight in bonfires you shall have your bellies full of them ere it be long—and if you live a week longer you shall see London as sad a London as ever it was since the world began."

This discourse was not taken much notice of at the time, but when the City of London was burnt, the said Henry Baker gave information to the said William Duckett, Esqr., who thereupon issued out his warrant to apprehend the said John Woodman; but he had fled the country, and could not be heard of afterwards.

This story is portentous, and casts the shadow of a dark imputation on the history of Chippenham, especially as "*the brave blades of the town were so fond of bonfires.*" And the alarming suspicion that Chippenham people had something to do with the Fire of London is strangely aggravated, and confirmed, by an astounding entry in the Borough Records——

"This year the Town Mill was burnt down—and EVERY MEMBER OF THE CORPORATION WAS PUT TO HIS OATH THAT HE HAD NOT SET FIRE TO IT."

There is the fact—dismal and ghastly enough—that the *brave blades of Chippenham were so fond of bonfires* that the whole Corporation of the Borough, the Bailiff and the Twelve Burgesses together, were under the foul imputation of having set fire to the Town Mill!——

RIOTS.

For ages the Town of Chippenham has been notorious for riotous assemblages of the populace. Soon after the Borough received its Charter, "*in the fourth and fifth year of o^{ur} Sovraigne Lorde and Ladye Philipe and Marye,*" certain persons were amerced by the Under Sheriff in the sum of £4.3.4. " upon certain riots and unlawful assemblies."

1630—Allusion has been made to the disturbance of the peace which resulted on the enclosure of Pewsham Forest.

Even under the stern despotism of the Commonwealth we read of some violent commotions, in which the mob attacked the military.

" 5 Jan. 1647——Another paper from the town of Chippenham recording a tumultuous rising of the people in those parts; they beat up the quarters of divers soldiers under Sir Thos Fairfax, and fell upon divers officers of the Excise."

About 1727—" a great company of those black disturbers of the peace (*i.e.* Colliers) came to Ford, and here with their hatchets proceeded to hew down a wooden turnpike gate; but notice having been given to Master Rogers Holland, who sitteth in the Senate for the town of Chippenham, that they were coming to pull down the gate within a short distance of that place, he took to his horse, and with his company well provided of swords and guns, said to the rioters—"*Render yourselves immediately*"——who threw stones, &c.; but eventually were sent under a goodly guard to the Chief Prison at Salisbury."

Sir Robert Long, of Draycot, writing, in 1740, about some riots in Chippenham, says—"*I am credibly informed that the Sheriff understanding how dirty and scandalous a thing it is, does not care to have it tried by gentlemen,* &c."——

On March 13, 1765, a notice with the Borough Seal was affixed to the Pillory that

"The Bailiff and Burgesses having maturely considered the ill consequences from the late unlawful Riots and assemblages consisting of a lawless Mob, any persons daring to assemble themselves in an illegal manner within 2 miles of the Borough shall be prosecuted."

On Aug. 5th, 1767, two Cheese Factors sued the Hundred of Chippenham at Salisbury Assizes "for a load of Cheese, value £60, forcibly taken from them upon the King's Highway by a company of rioters." The verdict was in favour of the plaintiffs.

A village revel used in old-times to be kept at Langley Fitzurse in the week following St. Peter's Day: it was, as John Aubrey says, "*one of the eminentest feasts in those parts.*" In 1822, this revel was the occasion of one of the "*eminentest*" riots in those parts. Some offence having been given at the feast to the villagers by a party of lads from Chippenham, on the 7th Sept. thirty or forty men from the two Langleys, armed with bludgeons, marched into Chippenham about 10½ *p.m*, went up and down the streets, shouting, calling the people to come out and fight, and attacking every one they met. The constables assembled, and aided by the men of the town, endeavoured to drive back the assailants, and a terrible battle went on for an hour or two in the dark streets—the constables were beaten down and wounded; one man died in a few hours; another shortly afterwards; and not less than thirty one men, women, and even children were more or less severely injured.

The chief actors in this savage and cowardly outrage fled the country: those who were apprehended, after a long confinement in Salisbury Gaol, escaped through an informality in the prosecution.

The months of November and December, in the year 1830, were a time of great alarm in Chippenham. Trade for many years had suffered great depression; wages were very low, work was short, and the agricultural labourers felt severe privations. Large mobs assembled in different parts of Wilts, and in the adjoining counties, and led by seditious men (not of the labouring class) burnt ricks, broke up machinery, and plundered houses in all directions: they were armed with axes, hooks, scythes, sledge-hammers, prongs, &c., and in some places amounted in number to a thousand men and women. For some days no force could be mustered in sufficient strength to arrest them. So severe was the strain, and so pressing the call on the Government for aid, that the Cavalry, Regulars and Yeomanry, had scarcely any rest, and were in saddle night and day, either guarding the gaols, or galloping off hither and thither to disperse the mobs before their numbers became great. Only one troop of Lancers could be spared on service in this neighbourhood, and they were stationed at Trowbridge, ready for any call, north or south, when they were suddenly summoned to gallop at full speed to Hindon, having received orders from Head Quarters to take no more prisoners, (as the gaols were full), but to ride down without mercy every man with a weapon in his hand. The Hindon insurgents, in formidable numbers, attacked the Lancers; three or four of the assailants were killed; hundreds were more or less wounded, many having their hands cut off when seizing the horses' bridles; and the march of destruction was arrested.

Meanwhile the storm of fire and ruin rolled onwards towards Chippenham, as near as Pewsham. The Magistrates sat continuously in the Town Hall; all the able-bodied men were enrolled as Special Constables, armed with the best weapons they could get, and they patrolled the streets all night. It was a time of awful suspense, as those few inhabitants of Chippenham well remember, who are yet alive, and took part in the proceedings. The country mobs were expected to enter the town every moment, and the Chippenham mob was ready to join them. The smoke of the burning ricks and farm houses at Pewsham could be clearly seen from Chippenham. Some of the constables had hurried home for a moment to say farewell to their families—when uncertain rumours reached the town that a fierce fight had taken place at Hindon, and that the mobs were severely punished. The cry soon ran to Pewsham—"*The Soldiers are coming!*"—the rioters dispersed—and Chippenham was saved.

Sir John Neeld and Mr. Goldney (afterwards Sir Gabriel Goldney, Bart.) were returned as Members of Parliament for Chippenham on Wednesday, July 12, 1865. The populace showed from the beginning of the contest much angry feeling in favour of Mr. Lysley, the unsuccessful candidate, but remained tolerably quiet on the day of election till darkness began to set in, when a mob of some 500 people, men, women, and children, assembled in the Market Place, and having overpowered the small force of policemen, proceeded to smash the windows of the houses, and destroy the property of the Conservatives in the town. The *Times* newspaper of the day, after recording riots in other places, thus reports of Chippenham—

"The palm of barbarism and brutality seems to have been reserved for the little agricultural and railway borough of Chippenham. The Liberal candidate having been defeated, a mob of five hundred persons assembled, and amused themselves for three hours in destroying the windows and furniture of the Conservatives. The house of the rector (Vicar) was assailed with tombstones torn out of his own churchyard, and a sick person who could not be removed from a front room* was protected by his servants who stood round his bed hold-

---

* "Fifty pounds weight of stones were thrown into this small chamber in a quarter of an hour. The houses ceased to be habitations, and became ruins."

ing up boards to keep off the stones. A butcher's shop was plundered as well as wrecked by the patriots, who did not forget their own domestic interests in their fury,—and to quell this riot, which had been long foreseen, only twelve constables were present. After all the mischief was done, a detachment of Guards was telegraphed for from Windsor; two hundred special constables were sworn in; and fifty fresh policemen were obtained."

The troop of the Yeomanry Cavalry from Calne also rode into the town. In most cases not a pane of glass was left in the houses. Shutters were wrenched off their hinges, and costly pictures, furniture, mirrors, chandeliers, &c. &c. destroyed. The damage sustained was enormous.

IX. THE MANOR OF OGBOURNE ST. GEORGE.

Twelve houses in St. Mary's Street, just beyond the limits of the old Borough, are said to have anciently belonged to the Manor of Ogbourne St. George, near Marlborough; and a tithing man was annually appointed to attend the Manor Court. Many years ago when an Act was passed to recover small Debts in the Hundred of Chippenham, these houses were exempted, nor could the inhabitants be sued, or their goods taken under an execution from the Chippenham County Court; and as late as 1834, when the Chippenham Improvement Act came into force, the rights of the Lord of the Manor of Ogbourne St. George were reserved.

One of the best ringers of the Parish Church of Chippenham, named Selman, having in some way transgressed the laws of the Borough, and in fear of the Bailiff's constables, fled into one of the Ogbourne cottages, and defied the Bailiff. The Bailiff withdrew his constables, and adopted a stratagem. Suddenly all the eight bells in the tower of the Church broke out in a merry peal. Selman, (without whose personal superintendence the bells were scarcely ever rung), thrown off his guard, suddenly rushed out of the cottage to listen to the unwonted sound; and was immediately grasped in the clutches of the law.

At present no Court is held at Ogbourne St. George, nor is it known by the land owners of that parish that the Manor ever possessed any property in Chippenham.

The cottages were probably leasehold or copyhold, and have lapsed to the Manor of Monkton.

X. *NOMINA VILLARUM.*

This document consists of returns made to writs of 9 Edward II. (1316) of the Towns and Parishes in every Hundred, for the military levies granted by Parliament to the King for furnishing *One Mark* (13s. 4d.) from every township, to supply soldiers for the invasion of Scotland. The original rolls became so worn and frayed by constant use that in I Henry VII. (1483) they were scarcely legible, and an order was issued early in the reign of Elizabeth that a transcript of *Nomina Villarum* should be made, and deposited with the Lord Treasurer's Remembrancer.

The volume was in the Lord Treasurer's Office in 1631, but has since disappeared; and at present no trace of it can be found. In 1800 it was supposed to be in the Exchequer, but might have been consumed in a fire. But copies, more or less perfect, remain, from which a fair draft may be executed.

HUNDREDUM de CHIPPENHAM.

Edmundus Gastelyn

BURGUS de CHIPPENHAM BUDESTONE	} EDMUNDUS GASTELYN.
SHERSTON COSHAM	} Maria soror Domini Regis, et monialis de Ambresbury.
SOPPEWORTH	Prior de Farley, et Johannes Mautravers.
COMBE COLERNE.	} Bartholomæus de Badlesmere.
KINGTON GRUTELINTONE NETELTON	} Abbas Glastoniæ.
HASLEBURY	Reginaldus Crok.
COKELBERGH	Henricus de Cobeham.
WEST KYNTON	Petrus fil. Reginaldi, et Cecilia de Bello Campo.
LITTLETON DREW	Walter Drew, et Johannes Pludel.

NOMINA VILLARUM.

LANGELE (Borel) . . LEIGH (De la Mere) . .	} Johannes de la Mare de Langeley.
SURYNDENE . .	Willus de Middlehope.
LOKYNTONE . .	Comes Lancast', et Thomas de Anerle.
YATTON . . .	Comes Arundel, et Henric de Lancastr'.
ALYNTON . . SLAGHTERFORD . .	} Prior de Farley.
BOXE . . .	Henricus de Boxe.
LACOCK . . .	Abbatissa de Lacock, et Johannes Bluet.
STANLEY . .	Abbas de Stanley.
BREMELE . .	Abbas de Malmesbury.
TUDERYNTONE . . (Tytherton)	Willus Percehay, Johes Tupin, Walt. Skydemore, Johes Kaleway.
WROXHALE . .	Johannes de Wroxhale.
HERTHAM . .	Johes de Hertham, Ricus de Comerwell, et Bartholom . Peche.
ESTON GREY . .	Johannes Grey.
SHERSTON PARVA .	Johannes Giffard.
HARDENYSSH . .	Johannes de Sco Laudo.
ALDRYNTON . .	Johannes de Hertham. Hugo de Davereswell. Robert de Harlegh.

XI. SHERIFFS OF WILTSHIRE.

Gentlemen in Chippenham Hundred and Neighbourhood who have Served the Office of Sheriff.

The Saxon governor of the Shire was the Earl. The Sheriff supplied his place. The SHIRE-REEVE is said to have been first appointed by Alfred, and it is gravely stated by Ingulphus that the moral influence of the new official was so great, that if a sum of money were left on the highway for a month, it would be safe. In some counties the Sheriff was appointed by the freeholders. In Wilts the office at one time was hereditary. The Judges now nominate three Esquires, and the Crown pricks one as Sheriff.

- 1163 MILO DE DAUNTESEY, Dauntesey.
- 1227 ELA, COUNTESS OF SARUM,
  Foundress of Lacock Abbey.
- 1304 HENRY DE COBHAM, Langley Burrell.
- 1345 SIR JOHN ROCHE, Bromham.
- 1356 THOMAS DE HUNGERFORD, Farley.
- 1374 SIR JOHN DAUNTESEY, Dauntesey.
- 1375 SIR JOHN DELAMERE, Langley Burrell.
- 1377 SIR PETER DE CUSAUNCE, Lackham.
- 1400 SIR JOHN DAUNTESEY, Dauntesey.
- 1402 WALTER BEAUCHAMP, Bromham.
- 1404 SIR WALTER HUNGERFORD, Farley.
- 1449 PHILIP BAYNARD, Lackham.

SHERIFFS.

1452 EDWARD STRADLING, Dauntesey.
1456 HENRY LONGE, Draycot.
1500 THOMAS LONGE, Do.
1502 WILLIAM CALEWAY, Titherton Kelways.
1503 SIR JOHN DANVERS, Dauntesey.
1511 HENRY LONGE, Draycot.
1515 SIR JOHN SCROPE, Castle Combe.
1522 SIR ED. BAYNTUN, Bromham.
1533 SIR WALTER HUNGERFORD, Farley.
1534 ROBT. BAYNARD, Lackham.
1544 ROBT. HUNGERFORD, Bremhill.
1546 RICHD. SCROPE, Castle Combe.
1547 SILVESTER DANVERS, Dauntesey.
1552 WM. SHERRINGTON, Lacock.
1553 EDWD. BAYNHAM, Lackham.
1557 SIR WALTER HUNGERFORD, Farley.
1565 NICHOLAS SNELL, Kington St. Michael.
1566 HENRY SHERRINGTON, Lacock.
1570 EDWARD BAYNTON, Rowden.
1573 SIR JOHN DANVERS, Dauntesey.
1574 SIR ROBERT LONG, Draycot.
1583 JOHN SNELL, Kington St. Michael.
1599 SIR THOMAS SNELL, Do.
1600 HENRY BAYNTON, Bromham.
1600 SIR WALTER LONG, Draycot.
1624 EDWARD READE, Corsham.
1628 JOHN DUCKETT, Hartham.
1629 SIR ROBERT BAYNARD, Lackham.
1631 SIR E. HUNGERFORD, Rowden.
1637 SIR E. BAYNTON, Bromham.
1644 SIR JAMES LONG, Draycot.

1664 SIR EDWARD BAYNTON, Bromham.
1718 GEORGE SPEKE PETTY, Box.
1730 EZEKIEL WALLIS, Lucknam.
1741 ANTHONY GUY, Chippenham.
1759 WILLIAM NORRIS, Nonsuch.
1763 JOHN TALBOT, Lacock.
1776 WILLIAM NORTHEY, Chippenham.
1777 JOSEPH COLBORNE, Hardenhuish.
1780 PAUL METHUEN, Corsham.
1787 ISAAC HORLOCK, Ashwick.
1788 ROBERT ASHE, Langley Burrell.
1791 JOHN AWDRY, Notton.
1792 MATTHEW HUMPHRIES, Chippenham.
1794 RICHARD LONG, Rood Ashton.
1795 JAMES MONTAGUE, Lackham.
1802 SIR ANDREW BAYNTON, Spye Park.
1808 JOHN HOULTON, Grittleton.
1819 JOHN LONG, Monkton Farley.
1820 AMBROSE GODDARD, Swindon.
1821 AMBROSE AWDRY, Seend.
1823 JOHN FULLER, Neston.
1826 THOMAS CLUTTERBUCK, Hardenhuish.
1831 PAUL METHUEN, Corsham.
1840 W. H. FOX TALBOT, Lacock.
1842 FRED. WM. ROOKE, Lackham.
1849 ROBT. P. NISBET, M.P. Chippenham.
1851 G. M. M. ESMEADE, Monkton.
1852 JOHN B. FULLER, Neston.
1854 EDMUND L. CLUTTERBUCK, Hardenhuish.
1865 T. H. POYNDER, Hartham.
1872 SIR JOHN NEELD, Grittleton.

SHERIFFS.

1874   E. C. LOWNDES, Castle Combe.
1876   W. H POYNDER, Hartham.
1877   RICH. WALMESLEY, Lucknam.
1878   GEO. PARGITER FULLER, Neston.
1885   C. E. H. A. COLSTON, Roundway.
1886   SIR H. B. MEUX, Dauntesey.
1887   MAJOR HENEAGE, Compton Bassett.
1889   J. E. P. SPICER, Spye Park.
1890   SIR J. P. DICKSON-POYNDER, Hartham.
1891   H. J. HARRIS, Bowden Hill.
1893   SIR G. GOLDNEY, Beechfield.

The Sheriff's Tourne, or Court, in olden days, was not usually held in any town, or village, nor even under any roof, but sometimes on the bleak open down, near an ancient cross, or old mere stone, under some great oak or elm, or on the boundary line of the Hundred, wherever the Courts had been customarily held from remote Saxon times.

There is at Longleat an original Latin record of the circuit of the Sheriff through Wilts in 1439 (17 Hen VI). The duty of the Sheriff of Wilts was to collect taxes due to the Exchequer, and to take cognizance of some petty offences. A jury was sworn, and presentments made by the constables.

For the Hundred of Chippenham, the Sheriff held his Court at Chippenham, after the Feast of Sts. Tibertius and Valerian.

XII. MAUD HEATH'S CAUSEWAY.

It is an exceptional incident that a town should be benefited by two such public paths as the Borough Causeway on the south, and Maud Heath's Causeway on the north, of Chippenham. The first, through the Forest, was a creation of paramount necessity; is as old as Chippenham itself; and was made and repaired by the Borough—the second dates from the end of the fifteenth century; was constructed at the cost of a private individual, and has ever since been supported by her benefaction.

MAUD HEATH deserves honourable remembrance amongst the benefactors of Wilts. About the year 1474 (13 Edward IV.) she devised houses and land in and near Chippenham to certain Trustees, who were empowered to form a raised Causeway (or as it is always called—Causey—) from Wick Hill, in the parish of Bremhill, to the limits of Langley Burrell, adjoining Chippenham. Her will, (or rather the document which constituted her will) is a narrow slip of parchment, in Latin, containing about six lines. She was a widow, and is always spoken of as, of Langley Burrell. The tradition is, that being a market-woman (though she herself never could have had much difficulty in travelling from Langley Burrell to Chippenham market, yet) she had regard to her friends from Bremhill and the neighbouring hamlets who were wont to flounder, basket, butter, eggs, and market-women altogether, in the perilous plashy flats, inundated by the river Avon.

Therefore of her bounty she provided a safe, dry pathway for all travellers in all weathers, through all time. The length of the Causeway is 4½ miles. It begins on Wick Hill, near a pillar, inscribed——

"FROM THIS WICK HILL BEGINS THE PRAISE
 OF MAUD HEATH'S GIFT TO THESE HIGHWAYS."*

On the neighbouring eminence, (which affords a magnificent prospect), stands a column crowned with an effigy of Maud Heath, in a sitting posture; on her head a heavy *coiffure*, in her hand a staff, and by her side a basket. An inscription attests that the memorial was raised by Lord Lansdowne and Canon Bowles, who added the lines ——

"THOU WHO DOST PAUSE ON THIS AERIAL HEIGHT,
 WHERE MAUD HEATH'S PATHWAY WINDS IN SHADE
   OR LIGHT—
 CHRISTIAN WAYFARER IN A WORLD OF STRIFE,
 BE STILL, AND PONDER ON THE PATH OF LIFE."

Midway of the Causeway, near the Bridge on the Avon, is another pillar, about 14 feet high, erected by

---

* Men have been grateful for other benefactions; hence a roadside seat called forth——

"GOD bless thee, Charley Anderson,
  For making here a seat,
That travellers may sit upon,
  And rest their weary feet."

—and a village well—

"GOD be thanked that William Pranket,
  In the year seventeen hundred and one,
Did cause this water here to run."

the Feoffees in 1698, with many inscriptions. On the south side——

"To the memory of the worthy MAUD HEATH of Langley Burrell Spinster* who in the year of Grace 1474 for the good of Travellers did in Charity bestow in Land and houses about Eight pounds a year forever to be laid out on the Highway and causey leading from Wick Hill to Chippenham Clift."

Underneath——

"INJURE ME NOT."

Yet the base names and initials of visitors disfigure the whole monument. On the east, south, and west sides are three Sundials, inscribed——

On the East——
VOLAT TEMPUS
Oh, early passenger, look up—be wise—
And think how night and day, Time onward flies.

On the south——
QVUM TEMPUS HABEMUS OPEREMUR BONUM.
Life steals away, this hour, oh man, is lent thee:
Patiently work the will of him that sent thee.

On the west——
REDIBO—TU NUNQUAM
Haste, Traveller, the Sun is sinking now;
He shall return again, but never thou.

At the extreme south end of the Causeway, where Langley Burrell touches Chippenham, there stood till within a few years, a stone pillar on a mound, which

---

* Her will designates her—VIDUA—*i.e.*—WIDOW.

was an important and noted land mark, and was known by name of CHIPPENHAM CLIFT. It bore a tablet with the inscription ——

   HITHER EXTENDETH MAUD HEATH'S GIFT
   FOR WHERE I STAND IS CHIPPENHAM CLIFT.

Both Pillar and Clift have disappeared. It was an act of apathetic barbarism (whether committed by the Local Board or Maud Heath's Trust) to subvert this ancient monument.

The destruction of "Chippenham Clift" is akin to that deed of crude Vandalism which utterly swept away almost the last memorial of ancient Chippenham by the removal of the Old Shambles.

The Feoffees to the Trust have usually been selected from among the gentry and clergy of the four parishes traversed by the Causeway, or of the neighbourhood. The value of the property bequeathed by the donor was, in her day, £8 a year. In 1834, when the Causeway fell under the inquisition of the Charity Commissioners, the Trust then held

			£	s.	d.
1.	Rent Charge on the Paddocks	.	0	14	0
2.	Ditto on Rowden Lane Close .	.	0	9	4
3.	Burgage House in Embry, yards, &c.	55	0	0
4.	Ditto Cook Street	.	18	0	0
5.	Two ditto St. Mary Street		15	0	0
6.	Ditto ditto Near Bridge	.	18	0	0
			£107	3	4

In 1611, the Feoffees had claimed a moiety of three parcels of ground which John Scott maintained had come to him through his wife; and he pleaded further that the Crown had also claimed them as Assart Lands of the Forest, and that he had compounded for them, and had secured a *mesne* conveyance from the King. A Commission at Malmesbury found the Feoffees' demand doubtful, and Scott was released on a rent charge of £1 . 3 . 4. for ever. Two tenements, mere cottages, had been let (being Burgage Houses) at an annual rent of £40 a year each. A general Election was impending. The feoffees offered a lease of their houses for 14 years at public auction, and obtained between £800 and £900. At this date they had five Exchequer Bills of £100 each, and a balance in the Treasurer's hand of £130 . 3 . 9., with arrears of £72 . 5 . 8—total £702 . 9 . 5. In 1811 they carried the Causeway over the lowlands about the channel of the Avon on a course of sixty four brick arches, and at a higher level than before; thus securing a passage above the highest floods known.

In 1853, at the joint cost of the County and the Trust, an Iron Bridge was thrown over the Avon. Up to that year a portion of the Causeway had never been finished—viz. that part from Langley Green across the Common to the foot of Pew Hill. By mutual arrangements the road down Pew Hill was now widened, and the Causeway completed in its whole length.

For many generations this noble pathway was of inestimable service, not only to the market-woman, but to the heavily laden packhorse, when there were no roads, or they little better than boggy tracks—but, as pitched with stone, (excellent for iron shoes, less suitable for soles of leather), the path, at best, was very hard and rugged. So that, as soon as good roads were made, the Causeway, from its very roughness, was abandoned, became useless, and was covered with grass. For the century last past it lay in such neglect and ruin that it was practically impassable, and it would be best described in Coleridge's verses on Cologne——

"Kölhn, a town of monks and bones,
  And pavements fang'd with murderous stones—"

The pitching, which cost £400 a mile, ought to have been replaced by gravel, which would have made a pleasant, useful path, at a cost of about £20 a mile. For the Causeway runs over a bed of gravel. But up to this day, except in two sections, the old, hard, cruel, barbarous pitching remains.

The Feoffees are chosen from persons who live miles away from the Causeway, and some of them may have never trodden upon it——while men of property who live on it, and are most interested in it, are excluded from all voice in the management.

It was undoubtedly the wish of the worthy Foundress of this Trust that her Feoffees should provide from time to time that kind of path which would be most useful and agreeable to pedestrians, most suitable and convenient to the public. The time is come when the intentions of the Donor of this valuable bequest should be carried into execution. The Causeway is a legacy—and the public (to whom the Causeway belongs) may insist that it shall, out of the abundant income available for its maintenance, be kept in good order, improved, and amended as the times demand; or application must be made to the Charity Commissioners to transfer the Trust to the County Council.

XIII. CHIPPENHAM during the CIVIL WAR.
1642 to 1645.

Sir Edward Baynton, of Bromham House, near Devizes, and Sir Edward Hungerford, of Rowden House, near Chippenham, were Members for the Borough of Chippenham in the Long Parliament: both at this time very hostile to the Crown. Of gentlemen in the immediate neighbourhood of Chippenham who rallied round the royal banner, were Sir C. Seymour, then residing at Allington (parts of whose mansion still stand) the Talbots of Lacock, the Scropes of Castle Combe, Hawkins of Hardenhuish, Howard of Charlton, Cleeter of Clyffe Pypard, Eyre of Chalfield, and Goddard of Swindon: but the name, which from the very first takes the foremost place in almost every dauntless adventure of those sanguinary days, and especially in the fierce struggles connected with the town of Chippenham, is Sir James Long of Draycot.

The head quarters of the Militia were at Devizes and Marlborough; both towns, like Chippenham, as yet open and defenceless. Of the military force then existent in Wilts, a company of foot mustered at Chippenham under Sir John Hungerford; and here also were the barracks of a light horse brigade, under Sir George Ivy. All the armed power in the county was under the dominion of the Parliament, who set Sir E. Baynton in supreme command. He posted himself at Devizes. But burning jealousies having arisen between him and Hungerford, his fellow M.P., the town and neighbourhood of Chippenham were long torn asunder by their mortal feuds. At length Baynton struck a daring blow. At dead of night, Lieut. Eyre, with six musqueteers, broke into Hungerford's chamber in Malmesbury, arrested him in Baynton's name, and had conveyed him some distance from the town, when the Malmesbury Militia overtook them, and released Hungerford. Baynton himself arriving in Malmesbury a few hours after, in his turn was seized by Hungerford, put into custody, sent to London, and cashiered from all his appointments in Wilts.

In March, 1643, Sir W. Waller entered Wilts; and this county for two years was the arena of several hard conflicts, in which he was one of the chief actors. As Wiltshire also lay in the main line of march between London, Oxford, and the west, it was crossed and recrossed by friend and foe in all directions, and the ungarrisoned towns, as was frequently the case with Chippenham, changed masters once or twice in the same day.

Waller, as Clarendon significantly notes, was not an enemy to tarry by the way longer than was needful. Passing through Salisbury, March 22nd, 1643, and leaving Devizes, as too strong, for another visit, he scattered the weak detachment in Chippenham, drove the King's troops out of Malmesbury, by a masterly movement captured Lord Herbert's army under the walls of Gloucester, and then summoned by startling news from Devon, turned westward, and for the first time met those gallant cavaliers of Cornwall, who were destined to inflict on him, in this neighbourhood, such signal disaster. After strenuous but vain attempts to prevent the advance of the Cornish army into Wilts, he posted himself on commanding ground on the north slope of Lansdown. Here he was attacked by Prince Maurice and the Cornish infantry, and a bloody struggle ensued, in which, amongst many other valuable officers, Sir George Vaughan, High Sheriff of Wilts, fell mortally wounded. Waller fell back on Bath, and the royal forces, seriously shattered, and anxious as early as possible to reach Oxford, broke up from Marshfield. They avoided Malmesbury, where Devereux, the Parliamentary general, was watching to spring out on any passing foe, moved on by Wraxhall and Giddy Hall, and had just reached Chippenham, when the skirmishers came galloping in with intelligence that Waller had come up by Box and Pickwick, and was threatening their rear with an overwhelming force. The royal generals at once drew the Cornish foot back out of the town, and offered immediate battle on the flat country, then but little enclosed, between Chippenham and Biddestone. But Waller, who as Clarendon again remarks, was a right good chooser of advantages, and whose strength lay chiefly in cavalry, dreading so soon to meet again those stern Cornish battalions on a fair field, declined the challenge, and the two contending powers stood to arms all night, in and around the town of Chippenham.

That Saturday night was a night of trembling for the people of Chippenham. None but children slept; none could tell whether the Parliamentary army might not force the river at some of the fords, and attempt to carry the town by storm. All night the streets rang with booming of cannon, the clash of arms, the tramp of steeds, and the heavy tread of the mailed soldiery. These were those stern warriors of Cornwall, who had left their homes in the far west, and sacrificing everything which the world holds dearest at the call of duty and honour, had held their triumphant way through Cornwall, Devon, and Somerset, routed every general the Parliament sent against them, scattered army after army, took fortress after fortress, and at last returned unconquered to their native country.

Sunday morning came, the 9th of July, 1643; Francis Dewy was vicar—he did not live to look upon the deadly strife in which his parishioners were doomed so often to take part. He died in September, the same year.

No fight actually took place that Sunday in Chippenham; the weight of the impending storm was reserved to burst with double fury on Devizes.

As the cavaliers left the town, Waller, with forces now considerably increased, immediately entered, and as soon as there was space on the south side of the town to deploy, launched his heavy horse on the compact columns before him. They were repulsed by Sir Nicholas Slanning, with the Cornish fusileers, but again and again returned to the charge. All through Pewsham forest, up Derry Hill, and along Sandy Lane, a running fight went on, till again Slanning turned and inflicted a damaging recoil—near Bromham Hall another desperate struggle took place, till fighting foot by foot, from field to field, and hedge to hedge, the harassed cavaliers with all their artillery, accomplished a safe lodgment in Devizes, on Sunday afternoon, July 9, 1643.

Waller encamped that night at Rowde, and on Monday morning marched all his forces over Roundway Down, and thus effected his long-desired object of putting himself between Oxford and the Cornish army. That evening, soon after night-fall, the cavalry cut their way in gallant style through the beleaguering host, and rode all night on the spur to Oxford. Tuesday, Wednesday, and Thursday, Waller made tremendous efforts to storm the town, and the small garrison, entrenched behind very imperfect defences, and exhausted by continual fighting, must soon have yielded at mercy, but that about four o'clock on Thursday afternoon the fire of guns, the fluttering of pennons, and the flash of sabres, announced the arrival of the Life Guards from Oxford. The Cornish foot burst over the barricades, and reached the field of fight just in time to see every squadron of the enemy's cavalry, and even Haslerig's stubborn cuirassiers, and all Hungerford's Western Horse, flying in tumultous rout before Carnarvon and the triumphant guards, over the dangerous precipices of Roundway Down. Lord Wilmot's reserve now joined the Cornish men, and overpowered the infantry who yet stood firm; and though Waller made every effort that a brave and skilful general could do, he was swept away by his own broken columns, and his whole army overwhelmed with irretrievable discomfiture.

It was late on Thursday evening when the people of Chippenham, who had distinctly heard the roar of battle, and from the higher points of view could catch the flash of the guns on Roundway, were startled by the shattered troopers of Waller's army, with Haslerig, Hungerford, and their general himself in the foremost ranks, thundering through the streets of the town, followed by confused masses of broken infantry, in dread of pursuit by the victorious cavaliers. There is an entry in the Church register, at this date, of the death of one William Iles, of Stanley, who it is recorded was killed in St. Mary's Street by a soldier.

On leaving Chippenham some of the fugitives took the road to Malmesbury, which was yet a Parliamentary garrison, the greater part continued their course through the night to Bath, but knowing the fortifications of that city could not long repel attack, pushed on to Bristol, where it is said Waller, riding up to the gates with a few jaded troopers, was the first to announce his own defeat—" My dismal defeat "—he bemoans in his memoirs—" the most heavy stroke of any that did befall me—I had nearly sunk under my affliction, but that I had a dear and sweet comforter—I did prove at that time that a 'virtuous woman rejoiceth her husband.'"

Leaving Hopton at Devizes, the Cornish army retraced its steps; an outpost was left in Chippenham: Malmesbury was occupied for a third time; Bath surrendered without any serious resistance, and in pleasant quarters, in that fair city, the Cornish troops rested from their severe service.

For the rest of 1643, and during the next year Wilts was unmolested, except that in May, General Massey, suddenly burst out of Gloucester, carried Malmesbury by storm, and, himself the only herald of his approach, broke through the slight earthworks which had been raised about Chippenham, captured a convoy of Royalists, passed on to Calne, there seized George Lowe, the Member, and still progressing in his daring raid, pounced upon the King's Commissioners in Devizes.

Massey occupied Chippenham as a temporary station, and barricaded, as occasion needed, Rowden House, Lacock Abbey, and other mansions.

Mr. Sherrington Talbot, lord of Lacock, had been taken prisoner and sent to London. Lord Hopton determined to secure Lacock Abbey, and accordingly sent thither Col. Jordan Boville with his own troop of horse. On reaching Lacock, they found it already seized by a detachment of Parliamentarians from Chippenham and Malmesbury. Boville rode on to Devizes, and taking hasty concert with Sir J. Long, it was determined without any loss of time, to attack Lacock. Advancing cautiously towards Chippenham, they received tidings by the way that Lacock Abbey had been abandoned, and that the strong garrison had removed to Rowden House, while a company or two were stationed in Chippenham itself. A troop of horse dashed instantly into Chippenham, and, amongst other prisoners, captured the Governor of Rowden. Thence they proceeded to Rowden, and summoned it to surrender. The only response was a volley of musquetry. A message was despatched to Bath to Lord Hopton to send up the heavy battering pieces. The artillery was immediately brought up by Sir F. Doddington, and a heavy fire opened upon the mansion. At the same time 400 dragoons arrived from Cirencester. But active measures were taken by the Parliamentary Generals in the district to raise the siege. Col. Stephens, Sheriff of Gloucestershire, burst through the royalist lines with horse and foot, bringing with him a much needed supply of ammunition and food. But while they rested a brief hour, and took some necessary refreshment, the busy foemen outside, aided by a number of zealous peasants from the farms and neighbouring town, cast up a huge barricade of earth, stones, and timber before the gate; "400 horse and foot were all cooped together, and the poor besieged were most desperately straitened by this kind of relief." Every hour made matters worse *within;* and the forces of the assailants, now massed together in the meadows to the number of 3000 or 4000, were increasing *without.* Suddenly Stephens, at the head of his troop, burst out of the great archway, accompanied by files of musqueteers, who by continuous volleys strove to drive back the besiegers, while others attempted to remove the barrier, so as to leave a passage for the horse. But the obstructions in their way proved too formidable—the whole sally was a disastrous failure—many fell dead on the rampart, and the rest were compelled to take shelter behind the walls.

The weather, however, (Feb. 1645) became extremely cold and tempestuous, and as the heavy storm for two days drove off the countrymen who were assisting in the works, it was hoped that in the confusion and darkness of night, the horse might break through; but the leaguer was so strictly maintained, Stephens saw that further resistance was fruitless, and he surrendered only on condition that their lives should be spared. Some of the prisoners of note were sent to Devizes; Rowden House itself was dismantled and set on fire.*

King Charles was moving to and fro in the county in 1644. He was probably in Chippenham in November.

Waller and Cromwell, then in a subordinate commission to Waller, were sweeping through South Wilts, when tidings reached them that Sir James Long, the Sheriff, with his fine troop (nearly all gentlemen) was at Devizes. Utterly unable to withstand the force arrayed against him, Long drew off precipitately by

---

* Many of the burnt stones of the old house may be seen built into the walls of the garden of the present farm; part of the moat remains, and the site of the foundations is easily traceable; and some of the buildings must have been left habitable, from an entry to this effect in the Church Register, eight years after it was destroyed—"A son of Mr. Herbert was born in some part of Rowden House, on Nov. 25, 1653, and died about two hours after the birth thereof."

the Bath road; but, by nightfall, the Draycot troop, which had done the King such signal service, was virtually annihilated, and Sir James, with twenty officers, taken prisoner.

On the tidings of this disastrous affray reaching Hopton, all the horse in Chippenham and other open stations were commanded to retire to Bath.

Sir James Long, after a few weeks' captivity was exchanged for Col. Stephens, who had been taken at Rowden. As soon as he was free, he hastened to his old quarters, rallied round him his old companions in arms, and on the 9th of May, 1645, burst into Chippenham, sword in hand. Overpowered by the fiery cavaliers, the scanty garrison was driven helter skelter along the narrow winding road to Malmesbury. They kept ahead, being mounted on fresh horses, through Stanton and Corston, until, after a chase of 10 miles, they ran in under the guns of Malmesbury, which, opening a rapid fire from the high ground, compelled the pursuers to retire. Sir James, however, had eyed some goodly oxen feeding in Cole Park: of these he selected 100 beasts, and drove them leisurely and safely before him into Devizes.

Bowood then belonged to the Audleys—but there was no mansion there. The Parliamentary Committee disforested the Park, and presented the deer to Sir E. Baynton, who, as a tradition runs, wishing to transfer these lively animals over Lockswell Heath to Spye Park, did so with the help of the clothiers of Calne and other towns, who formed a road of double skirtings of broad cloth, and thus drove them to their destination.

Many sanguinary skirmishes took place this summer in, and around, Chippenham. As often as the town was abandoned by the royalists, immediately a detachment from Malmesbury took possession. But, like Calne and Melksham, being a wide, straggling place, it required a larger body of troops than could be spared to defend it. In June, a large draft of men from Malmesbury, taking up the Chippenham detachment on its way, invested Lacock Abbey for a fortnight, and then made a furious effort to storm. They were beaten off with heavy loss, and fell back on Chippenham. Col. Boville, the Lacock general, in his turn, sallied out with Lord Hopton's horse, and ravaged all the country round, till one day venturing too near Chalfield House, which for a long time had been a stronghold of the Parliament, in an unguarded moment he was attacked by the infantry stationed there, and lost ninety-five horses. This was a most serious mishap: nevertheless Boville held Lacock, and entered heartily into a bold proposal to attack Col. Eyres in Chippenham. "They resolved," says the journalist, "to give Chippenham a sound alarm, and as that was answered to proceed further." On Aug. 12th, Sir James Long marched out of Devizes with a small company of fifty foot and a troop of horse, and joined Boville at Lacock. Boville's fragment of cavalry consisted only of twenty men—these he committed to Capt. Cook, and declaring he would never cross saddle till he had mounted all his men on rebels' horses, he marched on foot at the head of forty firelocks. The enemy had meanwhile thrown up some slight defences about the town, works, however, of so trifling a character, that one of their own journalists speaks contemptuously of Chippenham, as "an unknown garrison in Wiltshire." As the cavaliers proceeded stealthily on the road from Lacock, near the town they caught a stray soldier, and working on the fellow's fears, compelled him to confess that the works were weak, and insignificantly manned, and to divulge the more important fact that the cavalry had just ridden off in another direction. Without parley, Long and Boville attacked two breastworks with a narrow approach, soon cleared these barriers, and cut their way into the market-place.

Major Dowett, (hitherto one of the most dashing of the Parliamentary officers, but who had lately joined Sir James Long, and owned King Charles his lord for life or death,) charged at one of the main entrances, but his progress was long arrested by what is called in the journal of the day "a turnpike," but which was more probably some moveable barricade of timber work. Presumably Dowett's attack came by the Bath road—the only road from Bath into Chippenham was that narrow winding lane which now passes through Foghamshire. For an hour or two there was hard fighting at this point, and much blood was shed. Eventually the stockade was carried, and the enemy driven into the middle of the town, where they met Sir J. Long and his party, and fled along St. Mary street. A distant blast of trumpets gave them hope that their cavalry had returned, and expecting that the foe would be attacked from behind, they rallied, and for another hour made an effectual stand. In the fierce struggle to dislodge them, Dowett received a shot in the collar of his doublet, and the cheek of his helmet was blown off. Night only put an end to the savage strife. The victory was with the cavaliers. Some two or three hundred Parliamentarians escaped in the dark—others were driven into the river, and drowned—eighty were made prisoners—a quantity of ammunition was taken, and the Lacock captain redeemed his vow, and mounted all his men on rebels' horses. It is added that though the place was thus taken by assault, no plunder was allowed, and not a sixpence exacted of the townsmen.

It was not always so. Chippenham was plundered by Cavalier and Roundhead alike. Both parties mercilessly fleeced the unfortunate inhabitants. Col. Lunsford, the King's Governor of Malmesbury, inflicts a fine of £30 (=£100), and £10 for watching the Foss Road. Sir Ed. Hungerford (their own M.P.) exacts three rates in one year, besides bread, meat, hay, &c. Some fierce captain gallops into the trembling town with a peremptory demand for a month's pay for his troopers—another for a solid sum of £500. Sir W. Waller commands that a body of troopers, well-armed and mounted, shall attend him in the Market Place. Pikes, firelocks, armour, ammunition, corn, hay, food and money, had to be provided for the service of the Commonwealth, by a given hour: and Mr. Bailiff had no sooner wrung one contribution out of the pockets of the impoverished Burgesses than the call came for another; and sudden aud heavy penalty followed, if the subsidies were not forthcoming.

Later, in 1648, when General Cromwell himself came into the town, and put 400 horses into West Mead, (and spoiled the crop of hay for that year), he honestly paid £6 . 13 . 0 for one night's feed—*i.e.* 4*d.* a head.* And the townsmen rang the bells at a cost of 2*s.* 6*d.*, and gave him a bowl of sack and a bottle of claret, as he dined at the White Hart.

Some local and spasmodic movements in favour of the King were successful, but, before the end of 1645, the Parliament was triumphant throughout the Kingdom. Bristol fell, and all the West with it. Cromwell advanced on Devizes with a park of heavy guns, and Devereux laid siege to Lacock Abbey. Both places surrendered about the same time; and General Fairfax came down to receive in person the submission of the gallant little garrison of Lacock, and to salute their noble captain, as he marched out of the fortress which he had held so faithfully and so long. Lacock was the last post in Wilts held for the King; it yielded on Sep. 26th, 1645.

---

* But if Cromwell put his *horses* into West Mead, he seems to have put his *horsemen* into the Church—for we read in an old Churchwarden's Account Book—

"For mending a seat the soldiers pulled down   8*d.*
For making clean the Church which the soldiers defiled" . . . . 3*s.* 8*d.*

XIV. The Parish CHURCH of St. ANDREW.

THE first notice of a Church is in Domesday. Bishop Osborn, or Obern, held the Church of this Manor; it was endowed with land worth 55/- and, as the residence of a Bishop, must have been a position of importance even in the days of Edward the Confessor: and as Chippenham had been, for hundreds of years, the residence of the Kings of Wessex, some Church and hierarchy must have existed on this site from the earliest days of the conversion of the Saxons to Christianity.

The old Chancel, (arch and north wall,) was not later than A.D. 1120. It must have been built before any part of the Manor was alienated from the Crown; also before the tithes were impropriated, and while the Rector was yet resident. In the Chancel wall (N) were two original Norman windows, quite perfect, (filled with stones), and with fastenings for wooden louvres, showing that glass was not in use in the 10th century: one is retained in the new wall. On the outside of the Chancel was a Norman buttress of extraordinary breadth, supporting a 14th century staircase, which certainly did not lead to the Roof loft (as it would have crossed two windows) but perhaps to a Minstrels' gallery. The east and south walls of the Chancel were of the latter part of the 13th century. The Norman arcade, dividing the nave from the South aisle, was destroyed early in 1800. When the present Church was restored, in 1877, and a North Aisle built, no foundations of any former erection on that site were found. Yet it is hardly possible to believe that no North Aisle ever existed in so large a Church. The North wall of the Nave was rebuilt several times: once in the Commonwealth, in 1655, and again in 1801.

Mention is made of "Bayliff's Aisle," near the North wall. The first of that name, William Bayliffe, of Castle Cary, settled at Monkton, and, in 1632, made a vault, under covenant that he would pay a noble for every corpse interred in it. He died in 1652, and his was the first corpse for which a noble (*i.e.* 6s. 8d.) was paid. The roof of the nave was frequently renewed; the marks of three roofs remain in the Tower wall.

The Tower, and spire, were probably built, *temp.* Henry V. and VI. by Lord Hungerford, as his coat of arms within the Garter (and he was the only Hungerford who was ever a Knight of the Garter) is yet visible in the outer wall of the belfry. But the fine arch opening into the Nave, and the buttresses, testify of an Early English Church with a lofty, elegant spire. The Tower of the 15th century is said to have come to an untimely end through the propensities of the Chippenham people for bell-ringing. It was partly taken down in 1633, and re-erected with a lower spire, at a cost of £320, to which sum Sir Francis Popham gave £40. His arms appear above the Western door. In the Chancel, in Aubrey's day, was an altar-tomb of the 14th cent: part of this tomb seems to be inserted into the south wall. Behind the late reredos were found remains of pinnacles, finials, arches, and buttresses.

THE CHANTRIES IN CHIPPENHAM CHURCH.

CHAPEL OF ST. MARY. This Chantry, south of the Chancel, was built by Walter, Lord Hungerford, A.D. 1442, and endowed with £10 a year. With its large windows, its richly panneled parapet and buttresses *without*, and the sculpture, coats of arms, and profusion of gilding *within*, it must have been, in its perfection, a very splendid monument of mediæval devotion. Beautiful Early English arches divided it from the Chancel. It might have been raised on the site of an older Chantry. Near the Chancel arch was found half of a broken grave-stone, still a fine slab, bearing in low relief the figure (rude in art) of a lady under half a canopy, but on the dexter side; within a bordure certain Norman French words are barely legible.

ELE RR E ALIS SA FEMME FOVN-
DOYRSE VNE CHAVNTERIA A CEST
AVTER

This inscription may commemorate John Le Clerc

and Alice his wife. If Alice founded the Chantry, of her own pious bounty, she fills the husband's place on the memorial. In 1327, the Le Clercs had lands at Rowden, Sheldon, and Hardenhuish; it is possible they built the earlier Chantry. The present Chapel was covered with the Hungerford arms, but they are intermingled with those of the Beauchamps of Bromham, and others. In the S. E. angle is a monument to Andrew Baynton, who succeeded the Beauchamps, and lived at Rowden. A fine window was destroyed to receive Sir Gilbert Prynne's monument (1628) which monument is now affixed to the south wall of the nave. A "House of St. Mary" is noticed in Foghamshire.* Some lands belonging to the Chantry were bought by Henry Goldney at the Dissolution, and next century a Mr. Goldney was living in a house in St. Mary's Street, in the windows of which were arms of Beauchamp, Delamere, Rocke, and others. "*The Bayntons claimed a little manour of their own in or about St. Mary Street.*" (Aubrey). Later there was an Alms House there, for which the parish paid a chief rent to Sir Ed. Baynton. Edward the Sixth's Commissioners found in the Chantry——

"——a chalice silver gilt—vestments, amice and alb—2 candlesticks, cruets, altar-cloth, &c. &c. value 13s. 7d."

* In the chest in the Old Town Hall were found deeds of A.D. 1369, 1378, and 1380, signed with the Seal of the Borough, in which the Burgesses are described as 'Wardens of the Service of St. Mary in Chippenham.' and referring, amongst other tenements, to a house in High St., belonging to 'Our Lady's Chantry;'—abutting on the south side against Inchel's Place, alias Marshel's Place, (now Gutter Lane.)

The richer plate had probably been seized by an earlier commission.

CHAPEL OF ST. JOHN THE BAPTIST. This Chantry was attached to the Church of St. Andrew in Chippenham, but it is doubtful where it was situated. The endowment amounted to £5 a year—its altar cloths and vessels were worth 2s. 3d. at the Dissolution.

CHAPEL OF ST. KATHARINE. "The Fraternitie of St. Katharine" was a Society, or Guild, a religious Brotherhood, in the town of Chippenham, which had a Chantry of its own in the Parish Church for special Services, with an altar and Chaplain.

It is most likely that building, on the south side of the Church, which is now used as a vestry. This Chantry seems to have embraced a Guild Room below, and an Oratory above, approached by a winding flight of steps, still remaining. In the lower room a three-light Perpendicular window was laid open during recent repairs: and that chamber, having a door communicating with the Churchyard, would be easily accessible for the brethren, when they met for mere secular business. The Society possessed lands in Langley and Chippenham, worth £4.3.3 a year. On June 15, 1548, they had "2 vestments, albs and stoles, 3 altar cloths, 1 chalice* double gilt, cruet, bell and chest, worth 10s."

* The Commissioners reported that the Chalice was in the hand of Nicholas Snell—it was said otherwise that the Plate belonging to the said "Fraternitie of Saynt Kateryn" was in the hands of Mr. Pye. Mr. Pye must have been some very important personage in Chippenham, for his name appears also in Queen Mary's Charter, and in Leland's Itinerary.

In some way connected with the Parish Church were the Cantarists, or Chantry Priests, of St. Andrew—the names of nineteen priests being recorded, from 1333 to 1545. Whether they had a Chapel within the Parish Church, (the site of which is wholly unknown), or whether they executed certain religious offices in the Church apart from those services which devolved especially on the Vicar, it is impossible to say. None of them ever were Vicars, but they (the Vicars), and the Cantarists of St. Andrew and St. John were all nominated by the Prior of Farley. The Priests of St. Mary's Chapel were appointed by the Hungerfords.

THE VICAR OF CHIPPENHAM.

A Rector of Chippenham presided over the Church until about A.D. 1150, when all the tithes were severed from the parish by the Empress Maud, and bestowed upon the Priory of Monkton Farley, a Convent of Cluniac monks; the gift consisting of the tithes of the whole parish, including the Chapelry of Titherington, and that of Slaughterford.* This grant was confirmed by Henry II. The Prior of Farley appointed a Vicar. In 1534, Henry Myllyn, Vicar of Chippenham, deposed on oath that his benefice was worth in the gross £16.3.4 per

* A Jury found that the Church of Slaughterford " is not a Mother Church, but a Chapel annexed to the Church of Chippenham, which Church, with all its Chapels, Matilda the Empress gave to GOD, and the Church of the Blessed Mary Magdalen, and the monks of Farley."

an., but by payments of 4s. to the Archdeacon of Wilts and £2 to the Prior of Farley, his annual income was reduced to £13.19.4. The Bishop of Sarum had ordained the endowments of the Vicarage out of the tithes of Chippenham received by the Prior; but on the complaint of the succeeding Vicars, that their income was "*exilis (i.e. poor* and *insufficient)*, it was increased by Bishop Bingham, and again by Bishop De la Wyle, till the Prior of Farley protesting that the Vicar's income was "*immoderate*," a new award was made by Richard de Brankestone, official of Bishop Wykeham. The document is curious, and worth reciting——

"—— Whereas the Vicarage of Chippenham was endowed by the Prior of Monkton Farley, and whereas the Vicar's stipend hath been increased at divers times; yet, upon the Vicars complaining that their income was not sufficient for their maintenance and the burdens annexed, they procured their income to be *immoderately* enlarged; and there having arisen disputes between the Prior and Vicar; and they, being now desirous of walking in the way of peace, have submitted to our decree——

We, therefore, (being anxious to foster perpetual peace and tranquillity between men, and in order that the Author of Peace may be more and more devoutly worshipped in perfect love of hearts), do ordain and decree, that the said Vicar shall take and enjoy All the fruits and obventions of the Chapel of Tiderington in the aforesaid parish of Chippenham, (except the tithes of corn on Turpin's desmesne); and that the Vicar shall render 40 shillings a year to the Prior and Convent of Farley; and shall at his own cost provide for the service at the said Chapel by sufficient Ministers. Given at Sarum, Ap. 16th—Anno Domini 1272."

Thus the Chapelry and Rectory of St. Nicholas, Tytherton, with all their emoluments, became annexed to the Vicarage of Chippenham.

The Monastery of Farley received the tithes of Chippenham Parish until the Reformation, when (as stated before) the monastic estates were conferred upon the Protector Somerset. The Rectorial tithes ought to have been then restored to the Parish Church of Chippenham; but, by grant of Henry VIII. (two months before he died) they devolved upon the Dean and Chapter of Christ Church College, Oxford, with whom, since that day, the right of presentation to the Vicarage has rested.*

William Proudlove, Vicar of Chippenham, attests by terrier (29 Aug. 1608) that there belong to the Vicarage——

" A dwelling in Chippenham, with orchard, garden, and herbage of the Churchyard; the Easter book and Easter reckonings; the tithe hay in Westmead and other grounds; dues coming by marriages and churchings, and tithe eggs, throughout the Parish at Easter.

" At Titherton Lucas the Vicar hath a dwelling house, barn, garden, stable and bake-house; also twelve acres of glebe; the herbage of the Chapel yard; Commons for two kine one year, and for three the next; half an acre of

---

* In the Registry of " *Christ Church Evidences* " is this entry— (no date)—

" It appears there is no Howseing nor glebe land there (Chippenham.")

meadow; all the Tithe corn, grain, hay, and all other tithe whatever in Titherton."

On Feb. 10, 1766, the renewed lease of Chippenham great Tithes was assigned to Joseph Colborne for £3200 —the lessee was to repair the Chancel and Tithe Barn; and to pay £5 . 10 . 0 a year—probably an ancient pension —to the Vicar.

William de Avebury is the first Vicar of Chippenham whose name is recorded, in the reign of Henry III.

Since 1306 (34 Ed. I), when Alexander de Thornton was Vicar, to 1894, (if all their names have been registered) there have been 42 Vicars of Chippenham.

From the earliest ages of Christianity in Wessex, the whole County of Wilts formed part of the Diocese of Sarum. In 1836 the Ecclesiastical Commissioners severed North and South Malmesbury and Cricklade Deaneries from Sarum, and threw them into the newly-created Diocese of Gloucester and Bristol. South Malmesbury Deanery afterwards became Chippenham Deanery.

THE CHURCH LANDS.

The Church of Chippenham, in past pious generations, was endowed with many benefactions, chiefly in land.

Robert Trendlowes and Matilda his wife, daughter of Isabell, by deed of gift, dated 12th December, 1st of Henry *(no number)* devised on the Church of Chippenham two tenements and appurtenances in the High Street, called Coade's Place, and Waif's; a meadow called Trendlowes' mead, near the Avon; a close called Elmhey; a close called Odecroft; half an acre of land, and pasture for one cow in Cockleborough Field; and half an acre in Chippenham Field.

All the lands following, called Enford's, within the town and field of Chippenham, Langley Burrell, Cockleborough, Hardenhuishe, or elsewhere, viz.——

A tenement in the High Street; lands in the Cleve, Hendon, Rolnesdene, the Fleete, Odecroft towards Mouncton, Sanderditch, Bramellot-land, Mor Furlong, Nethercliffe, Westbrook-upon-Avon, Marbrook, Felditch, and the Clyne —measuring 13½ acres——
were conveyed to William Newman, Vicar of Chippenham, and others, on Nov. 21st, 11 Henry IV. by John Steere.

Thomas Fewre, St. David's Day, 33 Henry VI. conveyed to the Church of St. Andrew, Chippenham, a tenement in High Street, and three and a half acres of land in Hambreach, Poltingham, Ellford Theggs, Ballifmead, and Tolledown.

A messuage at Notton, in Lacock, called Seevey, was granted by William Sewal Stonford to William Newman, Vicar of Chippenham, and others, May 13th, in the 19th year of Edward IV.

A close, called Maggiscroft, in Notton, was demised by Thomas Godwyn to John Clerk, Vicar of Chippenham, and others, Nov. 1, 8 Henry VIII.

CHURCH LANDS. 151

In the first and second reign of Philip and Mary, 22nd Feby., John Panter bequeathed half an acre, called the Breach, abutting upon a pasture called Rowdens down, the lands of the Parish Church of Chippenham.

Concerning the houses and lands referred to in these bequests, a Vestry on Oct. 28th, 1638, empowered the Churchwardens of Chippenham——

——" To take course for the Discoveringe & recoverye of the ancient Church Lands, either by Suite of Law or otherwise according as by learned Counsell they shall be advised."

The result of this investigation is not recorded; but a note was made on a fly sheet of the Churchwardens' Book, which, after referring to certain enclosures, interchanges, and removals of the land marks of the "*ancient Church lands,*" and mentioning (amongst many like transactions) that " 184 *luggs in Sandy Ditch were given in exchange by Wm. Bayliffe, gent., to Mr. Scott, for which hee received satisfaction,*"—concludes with these ominous words—" *But the Church resteth unsatisfied.*"

The Charity Commissioners visited Chippenham in 1833-4, made personal scrutiny into the condition of the Chippenham Charities, and reported thus on the Church Lands——

" The oldest deed in possession of the Feoffees is a lease of all the Church Lands in May, 1696.

In the conveyance to new Feoffees in Jan. 1748, the property of the Church is described as

1. Tenement in High St. called GOD's Place.
2.   ,,   ,,   Old Building & garden.
3.   ,,   ,,   New Building.
4.   ,,   ,,   The Waves & garden.
5.   ,, near the Bridge with garden, together with 3½ ac. of land in Chippenham Fields, Poultingham, and Elford Tirling, and pasture in Home Breach, and Balls' Mead.
6. 5 ac. at Bolden, the Breach, Cockleborough Fields, (Ode's Croft) and Baswell.
7. A tenement, and close, and pasture for one Cow, in Cockleborough Fields.
8. Tremlows' Mead.
9. House, garden, orchard and field at Notton, called Maggott's Field."

The Commissioners proceed to say——

"We found it utterly impracticable to trace the property—some tenements remain in the hands of the Feoffees, but, with one exception, *the whole of the land is lost.* Most, if not all the land, whether arable or pasture, lay dispersedly in large Common Fields, with few or no marks to indicate boundaries, and no means now remain either of identifying the ground lost, or of ascertaining *when, or through whose fraud or negligence, the loss happened.*"

Thus the whole Parish of Chippenham lies under the bann of Sacrilege. This is the grim impeachment —that between the years 1748 and 1834, the Church of Chippenham was robbed of about 20 acres of its ancient inheritance; and this property must be in the hands of Chippenham families, whose ancestors perpetrated the dark deed, and on whom the aching curse that dogs sacrilege, now rests.*

The following schedule shows what part of its ancient heritages the Church possessed in the year 1834.

		£	s.	
1.	House in Market-place, rented at .	20	0	a year.
2.	Ditto ditto . .	20	0	,,
3.	Ditto ditto . .	34	0	,,
4.	Ditto in High St. ditto . .	12	0	,,
5.	Stables near Bear Inn ditto . .	6	0	,,
6.	Cottage, garden, orchard, and cow-leaze at Cockleborough . .	0	10	,,
7.	One acre and half of land on Bath Road	3	1	,,
8.	Cottage at Notton . . .	3	0	,,
9.	Ditto ditto . .	2	0	,,
10.	Field ditto . .	10	0	,,
		£110	11	

Most of the houses were in bad condition, and required large sums (*e.g.* No. 3 required £510 . 10) to put them into repair.

Respecting the income due to the Church from the wreck of the property, the Commissioners found that no regular accounts had been kept by the steward of the

---

* "Will a man rob God? Yet ye have robbed Me. But ye say, 'Wherein have we robbed Thee?' In tithes and offerings. Ye are cursed with a curse, for ye have robbed Me, even this whole nation." Malachi iii. 8, 9.

Feoffees, (who was also their treasurer), from 1803 to 1829, when he became bankrupt—and the Commissioners found, further, that the only times at which the Feoffees had met to audit the accounts, and to inspect the property, were in 1802, 1803, 1804, and in 1830. The Commissioners therefore appended to their Report this severe and merited censure——

"*We feel ourselves called upon to observe that we have scarcely ever known an instance of such protracted and culpable neglect on the part of a whole body of Feoffees, both with respect to the preservation of the property, and receipt and application of the funds, which it was their duty to administer.*"*

THE REGISTERS.

The oldest volume of the Registers is marked No. 2; it begins in 1578; it is named

"LIBER ANNALIS CHIPPENHAMI
CONTINENS NOMINA BAPTIZAT^{UM} NUPTOR'
ET DEFUNCTOR,' A FESTO NATIVITATIS DOMINI
1578."

It is bound in parchment, part of an old missal. It contains

Christenings } from 1578 to 1643
Burials
Weddings   ,,   1578 to 1616

* Report of the Royal Commission for Inquiring concerning Charities. 1834.

The first Christening registered is that of
"Christabell Stook de Tudrinton
bapt fuit xii° die Jan. 1578"

The first Marriage is—
"1579. Robert Tasker & Elizabeth Stephens
were joyned in matrymony xxij day of Januarie."

1587. An order is entered in the book to set down the names of the Fathers and of the Godfathers and Godmothers of the children christened, but it was done only once or twice.

The names of Bayliffe of Monkton, Barrett and Stokes of Titherton, Hungerford, Popham, Arch of Foulswick, Snell, Pleydell, Goldney, Ely, Seymour, Hawkins, Mountjoy, Rogers, Holland, Scott, etc. etc. constantly occur.

"1623. A stranger drowned in Avon was buried *in agro*."

" When I Henry Nash was chosen Clark by the whole consent
I straightway wrote these words incontinent
The vii day of Auguste as heere may be seen
In the 28th year of the Rayne of our Queen
Mr. William Chalfont being then Vycar, of this can Recorde
That was the date 1586 of our Lord."

"1638. John, son of John Scott, was baptized Oct. 7th."

[The following Document—unique as regards its date—should be found naturally in a Church Register; but it appears only amongst the Borough Records—

"The vjth daye of March Ao: Dni 1634.

"fforasmuch as Letters of Excommunication have bin latelie graunted forth from the Ecclesiastical Court of this Dioces against John Williams an inhabitant householder within this Boroughe wch were upon some Sabothe daye latlie past openlie read & denounced agaynst hym in this pshe Church of Chippenham whereby all psons are commanded and forbidden to come into his companye or to have anie comerce or dealing with hym: He the said John Williams is therefore thought to be a pson noe wayes capable at this tyme to have or receive anie benefit or pfitt out of the said Boroughe lands:

And therefore the daye and yeare last above written the said John Williams by the full and whole consent of the Bayliffe and Burgesses aforesaid or the greater pte of them assembled is utterlie debarred from haveing or receiving anie benefitt or pfitt at all out of the said Boroughe lands untill such tyme as he the said John Williams shall by order of the ecclesiastical lawes of this realme be restored & receid agayne into the Congregation of God's Church."]

Baptisms were regularly registered till the Civil War in 1642. After that year very few names appear in the Registers, but the Vicar, Jonathan Geare, never deserted his flock, and though he could not perform any Services in the Church, he administered the Sacraments in private to the few faithful ones who dared to receive them. Later on in the Register appears a long list of names with this superscription——

"Names of such as were baptized in the years 46, 47, 48, 49, 50; all which were registered by the then parish clerk, John Bond, in a small paper book." This is subscribed—"*Ita testor, Jonathan Geare, Vicar.*"—

Then follows this note in the Vicar's hand—

"*From this year till Sep.* 29, 1653, *the Register Book by reason of the discord in Church and State was neglected; in that year it began to be in use again.*"

In August, 1653, an Act of the Commonwealth passed, decreeing that a Registrar of Birth, Marriages, and Deaths, be elected; and accordingly Edward Berry, scrivener, was chosen for Chippenham; and irregular entries followed of Births, (not Baptisms), till 1558. In that year a page is headed in large letters—BAPTISMS of Infants—two names are registered in the Vicar's hand; and in 1659, a regular monthly record is made, each page signed "*Ita testor, J. G.*" till he died in 1680.

The gaps in the Register of Burials are very wide through the years of the troubles. In 1642 there are none from May to October; in 1643 some in Fr. Dewy's hand, the Vicar; he died in Sep. 1643; and no entry of Burials is made till Berry's appointment in 1653; then the entries are regular till his death in Nov. 1658, when they are continued by the Vicar, Jon. Geare.

The Register of Marriages of Chippenham is lamentably defective. For nearly forty years no record is extant. In 1653, the new Act came in force, and it is recited in full in the Register——Notice was to be given to the Registrar of the names, parents' names, and abode of parties proposing wedlock, and the same were to be published by the Registrar on three several Lord's

Days in the Church, Chapel, or in the Market Place, on three Market Days.——

Now for the first marriage. The contracting parties are George Sargent, of Nettleton, and Elizabeth Brown, of Chippenham; notice was given in Church on Dec. 4th, 18th, and 25th, at the close of the morning exercises, and no exception had. George and Elizabeth appeared before Justice Stokes, either at Capt. Taylor's, at the White Hart, or at the magistrate's own house at Tytherton Lucas, with two witnesses, who are examined on oath touching the premises—and then John takes Elizabeth by the hand and says:

"I, George, do here in the presence of GOD, the Searcher of hearts, take thee, Elizabeth, for my wedded wife; and do also in the presence of GOD, and before these witnesses promise to be unto thee a loving and faithful husband."

Elizabeth, on her part, now takes George by the hand, and says the same words, *(mutatis mutandis,)* with the additional word "*obedient*," as well as "*loving and faithful*." Justice Stokes then declares them to be man and wife—and they pay 12 pence. No other kind of marriage was legal.

There was express provision in the Act, that the Justice might dispense with the *pronunciation of words* in the case of the marriage of dumb persons, and of the *joining of hands* in the case of those who had no hands. A man might not marry before sixteen, nor a woman before fourteen years of age. At first the entries were made and signed by E. Stokes—later on there were no solemnizations. In 1659 nine persons were married, presumably in Church, as the page is subscribed, "*Ita testatur, Jon. Geare, Vicar.*"

The Corporation chest contains some parchments reciting the Declaration of the Bailiff and Burgesses against "The Solemn League and Covenant." The first of these documents now existing is dated 1679, and it is singular that the Declarations continued to be made, even after the Revolution, down to 3rd year of Queen Anne, 1705. It runs thus——

"In conformity to the late Act of Parliament made in the 13th year of our Sovereign Lord, Charles II. by the Grace of GOD of England, France, and Ireland, King, D.F."

"I, A. B., do declare that I hold there lies no obligation upon me or any other person from the oath, commonly called the Solemn League and Covenant, and that the same was an unlawful oath, and imposed upon the subjects of this realm against the known laws and liberties of the Kingdom."

THE COMMUNION PLATE.

A Chalice was left for the use of the Church by the Royal Commissioners in 1553, weighing nine ounces. This does not remain. It was probably replaced, in 1769, by two small silver cups, eggshaped, inscribed "*Deo et Eccl^{ae}* 1769. The same inscription appears on the Two Patens; Two Tankards, or Flagons, are inscribed "*Deo et Eccl^{ae}* 1769." A modern Chalice, of Elizabethan proportion and design, engraved with the vine and wheat-ears, was given in 1879.

THE BELLS.

They are eight in number. They were all cast by Rudhall, of Gloucester, in the year 1734.

They are inscribed——
1. Let us ring for the Church and King.
2. Peace and good neighbourhood.
3. Prosperity to the Town and Parish.
4. The gift of John Norris, Esq.
5. These bells were all cast by A. Rudhall, of Gloster.
6. Prosperity to the Church of England.
7. Unity and Loyalty. Saml. Martyn, Gent. Bayliffe.
8. John Norris. Esq. and Anthony Guy, Gent.
Churchwardens.

CHURCHWARDENS' RECORDS.

The "Account Book of the Parish Church of Chippenham" commences A.D. 1620. It is bound in parchment, a page of an old missal.

Chief rent for the Alms House paid to Sir Edward Baynton 2s. A new desk in the Reading Place.

1621. The Ringers on his Majesty (James I.) passing through the town . . . . . 10s.

Rate for relief of "poore Prisoners in the King's Bench Marshalsey, maymed soldiers and mariners, & the Gaole of Fisherton Anger" . £2 5s. 8d.

A cloth for the deske, a carpet for the communion table, a communion cup with gilt cover

1622.	A poore minister wanting means . . .	4s.
	A new Flagon bought	
	For mending the Church Bible and for the carriage of him to London	6d.
1623.	To mending leads hurt by a fall of a Pinnacle in a Tempest	1s. 8d.
	To the King's Majesty's Commissioners & Clerkes at Corsham at the Tyme of showing the Deeds of the Church lands	£2.
	To the Ringers on the safe return of the Prince (afterwards Charles I.) out of Spayne	
1625.	Book of Thanksgiving after the great Infection in London	12s.
	For destroying a want (*mole*) . . .	4d.
	For Bishop Jewell his apologie . . .	7s.
1633.	Of Sir Francis Popham, Kt. his gift toward re-edifying the Tower and Steeple . . .	£40.
	The Steeple taken down to the Tower	
	£320 paid for rebuilding the Tower and Steeple	
	A board for the Charnel house	
1637.	For painting the Kings Arms, 8 other Arms, and writing 24 sentences on the wall of the Church	£24 10s.
	Cleaning the Screene	
1633.	For levelling a quarr in the Churchyard	
1645.	For the head of a fox	
	The great bell new cast at Warminster	
1650.	The Ringers when Col. Cromwell came through the Town	2s. 6d.
	Do. when Newes came of routing the Scottes .	5s.

	Do. when Sir John Danvers his son (Henry Danvers) came . . . . 1s. 6d.
	For mending a seat the soldiers pulled down . 8d.
1651.	For making clean the Church which the soldiers defiled . . . . 3s. 6d.
	To Edw. Maundrell for defacing the Kings Arms 2s. 6d.
1655.	The walls of the N. side of the Church rebuilt
1659.	Digging the fives place . . . . . 1s.
	For carrying the hour glasse, for mending & bringing him again . . . . 5d.
1662.	The Ringers when the King was proclaimed 2s. 6d.
	For setting up the Kings arms . . . £5.
	To a gray (*Badger*) killed in the parish . . 1s.
	The surplice and hood . . £5 4s. 8d.
1677.	Pulpit cloth, cushion and fringe . . £3 18s.
	For a Hedgehocke . . . . . . 2d.
	For the relief of poor Christian Captives in Turkey £6 12s.

CHARITIES.

—— Bull gave £20 to be lent out to tradesmen and apprentices in sums of £5 each.

Sir Henry Baynton left £20 to be lent to poor artificers in sums of £6 . 13 . 4 each.

Richard Woodland gave £5
Richard Pearse (1623) gave £5
Walter Gale (1627) gave £2   } on loan.
Wm. Proudlove, Vicar, (1630) gave £2
Thos. Hawkins (1639) gave £10

1642. Adam Milshum left £10—the interest to be applied to the repairs of the chimes of the Church.

All the above bequests are lost.

In 1615, Thomas Ray, of New Sarum, gave his dwelling house and thirteen small tenements in Sarum for the benefit of poor clothiers of Trowbridge, Chippenham, Westbury, and Marlborough, in turns.

In 1628, Robert Gale, vintner and citizen of London, left £20 a year to be distributed by the Bailiff and Burgesses to deserving poor at the Parish Church—a preacher to have 20/- for a sermon, and the Bailiff and six of the ancientest Burgesses to have 20/- to drink withal for their pains. For many years all the deserving *second* poor of the whole parish received a half crown each.

Mrs. Hawkins, of Chippenham, in 1688, left the interest of £10 to be paid by the Bailiff to six poor Widows of Freemen.

Henry Smith, formerly citizen and silversmith of London, in 1642, left estates to the Governors of Christ's Hospital for the benefit of twenty-three parishes, (of which Chippenham was one), that certain rents should be expended for the relief of impotent and aged poor in the purchase of clothing of one colour with some badge by which the donor might be remembered—or else, in the distribution of bread, flesh, or fish on every Sabbath Day publicly in the Church.

In 1681, Gabriel Goldney charged his lands at Tytherton with a payment of £6 a year to provide coats for six honest labourers.

John Wicks, gent, of Chippenham, in 1687, gave eight acres and a half of land in Pipsmore Field, to the Minister and Churchwardens, to provide clothing for the people of the town where there was most need.

In 1735, Sir Francis Popham, demised 14ac. 1r. 10p. of land at Foxham, in the parish of Christian Malford, to the town of Chippenham, the rents of which lands were to be divided among six poor freemen, whom Sir F. Popham, and his heirs, might nominate; or in default of such nomination, such as the Bailiff and body corporate might appoint.

By the recitals contained in a deed of appointment of new trustees to the Freemen's Charity, Aug. 30, 1781, it appears that £1000 had been invested by William Colborne in the purchase of £1100 3 per cent. Consols, standing in the names of Sir James Tylney Long and other trustees, upon trusts declared in a deed of Nov. 17, 1769. The trusts of the deed of 1769 were such that the dividends of the £1100 should be applied to the benefit of such freemen, or freewomen, of the borough of Chippenham, in money, clothing, or provisions, as the trustees should think fit. Latterly all the distributions were in money, of sums from ten shillings to three pounds, according to the needs of the recipients.

Ann Bradbury, in 1834, left the interest of £100 to be laid out in blankets, provided that every fifth year the interest be reserved, and expended in the restoration of her sisters' tomb.

Robert Sadler, in 1838, bequeathed the interest of £300 for buying drab cloaks for old women, provided that his own tomb was always kept in repair.

In 1842, Rebecca Church bequeathed the interest of £304 to be expended in the purchase of duffel coats for poor women.

In 1851 William Gundry left £500 in trust to the Vicar and Churchwardens to expend in the purchase of coals or clothing.

MONUMENTAL INSCRIPTIONS.

(Before the Church was restored in 1878.)

Near this place lyes interred the Bodies of Anthony Martyn gent. who died on the 19th day of March 1719 in the 61st year of his age. His Wife Mary Martyn expired the 17th of April 1731 aged 70 years.

Robert Martyn of the Inner Temple Esq. their only son died 12th August 1733 in the forty forth year of his age. In whose Memory this Monument was erected by Mildred Martyn his Relict. Also Mildred Wife of the above Robert Martyn Esqr and Relict of Rogers Holland Esq departed this life 28th of January 1776 in the 77th year of her age.

Neare this place lyeth ye body of Mary ye wife of Thomas Chappell of this Bvrrovgh clothier & davghter of Mr Tho Andrews Minester of God's word late of Shaston in Dorset who departed her life the j5th day of February Ao j689.

Noe sooner are we borne to live then dy,
Ovr first day doth assvre vs of ovr last,
Whilst evry moment we doe hasten ny
To ovr longe home, and w'have liv'd is past;
For man to live here ever cannot bee;
Longe to enjoy we mvst not think. A change
Attends vs and thov groneing wail'st to see
That day, Dear Sovle, life here at last seem'd strang,
'Twas sicknes, now thot liv'st when death hath wrovght
Its malice and soe ended hath all greif;
Happy be those mishaps which thee have brovght
A gaine fvll los and in thy death a life.

Here lyeth the bodye of Alice the wife of Thomas Longe Gent: late deceased shee departed this life the 17th day of November ano Dni 1641.

Reader beholde what little staye or trvst
Is to bee sett on man whose strength is dvst;
Consider well thye brittle state on earth,
How everye moment's svbject vnto death;
Amend then what's amiss thy sins forsake
Repent in tyme peace in thy conscience make;
Death spareth none yet when hee strikes or how
For man before hande 'tis too mvch to know.

Richard Foreman late one of the Bvrgesses of this Borough departed this liffe the 25th day of March ano Dni 1639 whose body here lyeth bvryed.

Erected in commemoration of William Pew gent: and Grace his wife, the said William departed this life October 31 ano Dom. 1648, and Grace departed this life the 25th of Avg. 1635 whose bodies lie here in terred. Moriendo vivimus Vpon the death of Mr William Pew and Mrs Grace his wife bvried in the same grave.

Behold my grave is now a nvptiall bed
Whom once on earth in earth I now doe wed
Wth chaste embraces death was not vnkind
To part vs so that shee may stronger bind;
No reader now ovr blisse is near complete
For here ovr dvst above ovr sovles doe meete

Here lyeth the Bodye of Alice Hawkins Daughter of Robert Hawkins late of Hardenhuish Clothier Shee departed this life on the 31st of Aug. 1657 ætat suæ 29

> Nuptiæ replent terram
> Virginitas Paradisum. Amb.

Here lyeth the body of Thomas Hawkins Gent. late one of the Bvrgesses of this Borough who departed this life the 4th day of December ano do. j676.

> The father and two sones united be,
> This grave containes whats mortall of ye three;
> The mother also near to those doth ly,
> Whose sovles no doubt enioyes felicity.

In memory of Lewis Purbrick, M.A. 23 years Vicar of this Parish, and Rector of Tytherton Lucas near Chippenham, who died 26 Augt 1860, Aged 55 Years. Also of Anna Purbrick, His Sister, who died 25 May 1840, Aged 31 Years, Mary Purbrick, His Aunt, who died 19th Octr 1847, Aged 72 Years. Hannah Purbrick, his Mother who died 18 April 1849 Aged 81 Years. Sarah Clarke, His Aunt, who died 24 June 1855, Aged 81 Years. All buried at Tytherton Lucas. Also of Emma Purbrick, His Sister, who died 7 Feb. 1881, Aged 76 Years. Buried in St. James' Cemetery, Bath. Also of Mary Anne Catherine Parker, His Sister, who died 14 Jany 1882, Aged 79 Years. Buried in the Cemetery, Ealing.

A large altar tomb inscribed on top

> Armiger hoc tvmvlo iacet hic gencrosvs opaco
> Andreas Baynton qvi nominatvs erat,
> Qvem genvit miles bene notvs vbiqve edovardvs,
> Hvivs erat heres nvnc requiescit hvmo.
>   Ao Dm. 1570.

Here lieth the bodie of Thomas Hungerford the sonne of Anthony Hungerford of the Lea, gent. who departed this life August 15th, 1665 aged 22 years.

Near this place lyeth the Body of Elizabeth, the wife of Jonathan Scott, gent, late of the Ivy, who departed this life the 25th day of April, Anno Domini 1718, Aged 77 Years.

Near this place lyeth the Body of Mr. Jonathan Scott, of ye Ivy, who departed this life ye 28th day of Jan., Ano Dom. 1693/4, Aged 85 years.

Juxta hunc Lapidem Jacet sepulta Elinora, uxor Jonathanis Scot, de ive. hujus Parochiæ, Filia Henrici Bayliffe, nuper de Chippenham, arm. quæ obdormivit 4 die Februarii 1664, Anno Ætat: suæ 61.

    Quæ modo peccatis mundi vexata dolebat,
    Jam Christo et Sanctis consonat illa Deo.

Here Lyeth the Body of John Brookes, who departed this life the 7th of Dec. A.D. 1722, Aged 82 years.

Maria, ux. Johannis Brookes, filia Domini Thomæ Fereby, de Episcopi Cannings, nuper Vicarii dignissimi, decimo septimo die octobris mortua, 19º ejusdem mensis 1666 sepulta.

    Cara deo, dilecta piis, pretiosa marito,
    Vicinis, lenis pauperibusque fuit.

On the Floor.

Here lieth the Body of Jane, the wife of Jonathan Scott, who died Jan. 2d 1774, Aged 44 years.

On Floor of South Aisle.

In Memory of Elizabeth, Wife of George Scott, who died July the 28, 1733, aged 45 years. Also, Walter, son of

George and Eliz. Scott, died April 20, 17....years. Likewise two of their daughters died infants.

Here Lyeth ye Body of John Wastfield who dep. this life Aug. 11, A.D. 1741, aged 40 years. Also here lyeth the Body of Edward Wastfield, who departed this life March 11 A.D. 1742, aged 33 years.

William Grinfield, Esqr died August ye 17th, 1762, aged 61 years.

Here lyeth ye Body of Martha, the Daughter of William and Mary Gale, who deptd this life the.... day of June Ano Dm, 1724.

Sarah Coke died May ye 17th, 1777, aged 50 years.

Here lieth the Body of Anne, ye Wife of Samuel Marten, who exchanged this life for a better, September ye 2nd A.D. 1731. Also Samuel Marten died June ye 8, 1749.

John Holland, aged 21 years, A.D. 1740. The Rev. Christopher Holland A.M., 22 years Vicar of this Place, died May ye 8th 1760, aged 52. Elizabeth, Wife of the above Christopher Holland died April 28, A.D. 1746, aged 72 years. Nicholas Trueman Esqr died April ye 2d 1778, aged 64 years.

Here lieth the Body of John Jennings, Gent. who died July ye 3d 1795, aged 70 years.

In Memory of Sarah Allen who died the 5th of Nov. 1769 aged 27 years. It was not requested (*sic*) to be deposited here with her truly affectionate friend Frances Batchlor, Wife of Mr George Batchlor of North Bradley in this County and sister to Mr Jennings, Surgeon of this town. She died the 26th of October 1776 aged 44 years. Also Mary Jennings, died Sept. 29, 1792, aged 75 years.

......Alice Hawkins......*Brass taken out.*

Willim Ballenger who died Novr the 26, 1815. aged 56 years.

John Warne died Octr 13th, 1759, aged 38. Elizth Jones Daughr of Roger & Elizth Warne died Octr 5th, 1782, aged 43 Elizth Wife of Roger Warne died July 2, 1765, aged 78. Anna, daughter of John & Eliz. Warne, died April 22, 1787, aged 27 years. Mary, wife of Archibald Litle, gent, who died Nov. 20, 1799 aged 42 years. Elizabeth, wife of John Warne, she died July 13, 1802, aged 74 years.

In Memory of Mary, wife of Thomas Sparrow, who died Sept. 22nd, A.D. 1763, aged 41 years. Also in memory of Thomas Sparrow, who died Nov. ye 6th, A.D. 1771, aged 88 years. Also in Memory of Ann, wife of Thomas Sparrow, who died April 15, A.D. 1777, aged 82 years.

In Memory of George Stucley who died Feb. ye 23d, 1755 aged 44 years. Also here lyeth the Body of George, son of George and Margaret Stucley, who departed this life the 7th day of Sept. A.D. 1763, aged 19 years and 6 months.

In Memory of James Barnes, who died Dec. ye 25th, 1744, aged 57.

In memory of Abraham Noble, gent. of Maldon in the county of Essex, who departed this life March 11, 1748, aged 57 years.

William, son of Wm. and Margaret Lovegrove, died February 22nd, 1743, aged 16 years. Margt Lovegrove died March 21 1757, aged 67 years. Also Margaret Lovegrove, spinster, died June 10 1802, aged 70 years.

William Lovegrove died Feb. ye 18th 1778, aged 84 years. Also Ambrose Lovegrove died June ye 23rd 1788, aged 66 years. Also Mary, Relict of Ambrose Lovegrove, died Sep. ye 9th 1800, aged 81 years.

Underneath this stone lies interred the Remains of Ann, wife of Richard Smith of Rowdendown, who died March the 22nd, 1770, aged 63 years. Also Richard their son, died March the 8, 1774, aged 32 years. Also Richard Smith who dep. this life March 6, 1777, aged 70 years.

Francis Hill Verchild, wife of Lewis Brotherson Verchild (of the Island of St. Christopher, in the West Indies), departed this life 20th Sept. 1810.

In memory of William Gale, son of Wm. and Eliz. Gale, who died Nov. 24, 1754, aged 5 months. Also Mary, their daughter, died May the 27, 1765 aged one year. Here lieth interred the Body of Eliz., the Wife of Wm. Gale, who died ye 13 day of Nov. 1769, aged 40. Also the Body of the said Wm. Gale, gent. died Jany. 18, 1800, aged 72.

In memory of John Wilson, son of Stephen and Mary Wilson, who died Oct. 26, 1764, aged 74 years.

Here lieth ye Body of John Dunn, who died June the 17, A.D. 1760, aged 84 years. Also here lieth the Body of Ann, wife of John Dunn who died Nov. the 13, A.D. 1760, aged 74 years.

Here lieth the Body of Catherine, wife of Joseph Colborne, who departed this life June 16, A.D. 1753, aged 65 years.

Here lieth the Body of Jane, wife of Joseph Colborne, who died Sept, ye 3, 1755, aged 28 years. Also Jane, daughter of Joseph and Jane Colborne, who died March 3, 17. .aged 3 years.

In memory of Ann, wife of Thos. Holmes, who died July ye 8, 1764, aged 47 years. Also in memory of Thos. Holmes who died May ye 8, 1788, aged 84 years. Also Elizabeth, wife of Wm. Bowsher, died Jan. 12, 1816, aged 59 years.

Here lieth the Body of John Emmett who departed this life the 12 of Nov. 1711, aged 52 years. Here lyeth the Body of Margaret, the wife of Nicholas Emmett, who departed this life Sep. 13, A.D. 1716, aged 65 years.

Here lyeth the Body of Eliz., wife of Joseph Colborne, who dep. this life 14 day of Feb. A.D. 17.... aged 21 years. Also here lyeth the Body of Joseph Colborne, Burgess of this Borow, who dep. this life Oct. ye 7, 1734, aged 51 years.

Near this place Lyes interred the Body of Mr Gilbert Lake, B.D. who was formerly Student of Christ Church, in Oxford, and 15 years Vicar of this place, the Income of which he had the pleasure of Augmenting by procuring

One Hundred Pounds from Mr Colston, and adding One Hundred Pounds more of his own to Queene Ann Bounty. He also built Part of the Vicaridge House. He was the Son of the Rev. Mr Wm Lake, formerly Student of the same Colledge, and Vicar of the same Place. A worthy son of so worthy a Father, who having finished his Allotted time of Trial here, Departed this life in the 48th year of his Age, and of our Lord 1740.

In spem beatam Resurrectionis juxta dormit Gul. Lake, A.M. Ecclesiæ Hujus Vicarius dignissimus, Sarum Præbendarius, Ædis Xti, Oxon., olim alumnus, omnibus ibidem Semper Charus, qui post annos 23 In ministerii munere illibata pietate, incorrupta fide, candore et prudentia singulari, Indefessa et felici diligentia peractos, de omnibus bonis bene meritus flebilis, ob. 9_o die Martii, A.D. 1703, Ætatis suæ 57.

Johannes, fil. Jonathæ Rogers, gen: et Eliz: ux: ej: obiit xx die Decembris 1674. Maria ux: Jonathæ Rogers, gen: .... fil. Nath. Long de Langrish .... Hanton, Ar: ob: 3º Sep. Aº Dom. 1711.

Elizth ux: Jonathæ Rogers, gen: et filia Anthony Saunders, S.T.P. obijt nono die Feb. A.D. 1619 *(sic)* Eorum filia Margareta obijt 1673. Hic conditæ jacent Reliqiuæ Jonathæ Rogers, gen. qui obijt 30 Aug.

Anno { Ætatis 82.
{ Salutis 1715

Josephus, filius Johannis Holland, arm. obijt die Februarii....1780.

Elizth, filia Jonathæ Rogers, Gen. obijt secundo die Aug. 1677.

Johannes Holland, Ar. obijt 26 Aprilis Anno Dom. 1723. Ætat 52.

Dorothæa, ux. Johis Holland, Ar. obijt 20 Aprilis, 1726, Æt 51.

Here lyeth Jane, the daughter of John and Mary Merewether, who was born June the 8, 1729, and died Oct. the 31, 1731. Also Eleanor, their Daughter, who died Dec. 6th. A.D. 1739. Also William, their Son, who died May the 17, A.D. 1741. Also Edward, their Son, who dyed February 13, A.D. 1745. Also William, their Son, who died June 19, 1747.

Here lyeth the Body of Mary, wife of John Merewether, who died July 12, 1756, aged 50 years.

Hic jacent Ossa Viri Desideratissimi, Johannis Merewether, M.B., Ædis Christi apud Oxonienses olim Com., qui nullius interim seu boni Civis, seu Patris familias, Officii immemor Medicinam miseris Levamen: Haud minori Liberalitatis quam Ingenii Laude, annos amplius quadraginta In hoc Municipio feliciter exercuit. Obiit Maii 24, Anno Domini 1774, Ætatis suæ 88.

Richard Pocock Senr died August the 21, 1777, aged 68 years. Also the Body of Sarah, wife of Richard Pocock, who departed this life the 26 day of May, 1781, aged 32 years. Also in Memory of Jane, the wife of Richard Pocock, Senr. who dep. this life the 21 day of May, 1785, aged 76 years.

Here lyeth the Body of Mary, wife of Richard Lewis,

of Corsham, Esq., and Daughter of Giles James, of Sherston-Pinckney, gen; Aged sixty years who dep. this life ye 27 of Feb. Anno Dom. 1697.

In Memory of James Hall, who died Dec. A.D. 1750, aged 35 years.

Roger Warne, Gent: died June 5th, 1773, aged 85. To the Memory of Mrs Eliz. Warne, spinster, born in 1686, and died in Jan. 1763.

Sarah, ye wife of Henry Singer, gent., died Sept. 9th, 1775. Henry Singer, gent., died Oct. 18, 1778, aged 70.

Bazilla Chappall died Feb. 22, A.D. 1752, aged 61 years.

Here lieth the Body of Wm Bradbury, who departed this Life Dec. 24, A.D. 1763, aged 43 years. Also of Clementina, his wife, who departed this life Dec. 27, A.D. 1785, aged 63 years.

Franciscus Cock, Arm. Roberti fil. Et Pater Ex Agro Norfolciæ, Hic Dormit; qui hæc Dormiens Verba facit, Nam Somnians et vigilans semper erat Mortis Memor, Cœlo natus Cœlum spiro, mundum calco Ressurrecturus. Doctrinæ felicissimus amator. Theologiæ præcipue scientior, Regis et Ecclesiæ Defensor, Religionis asiduus cultor, Peccantes Liberrime arguit, Temperantiam, Fidem, Patientiam, Dictis facto Commendavit, A terrenis se abstraxit; Alios ad Superna excitavit, Omnibus ut posset profuit.

{ Obijt Anno salutis 1704 } Jan. die 11º.
{ Ætatis autem suæ 81 }

NORTH CHAPEL.

Here lyeth the Body of Elizabeth, ye wife of Richard Long of this parish, Gen: who died the 22nd of Octo: Anno Dom. j69j. Ann, the wife of Thomas Long, Esqr, died Oct. ye 24, 1724, aged 72. Also Mary, wife of Thomas Long, Esqr, who died July the 6th, 1773, aged 72 years.

LONG of Monkton. H. S. Thomas Long de Rowden, Gen: qui obijt 21º Maij, Anno Dom: j69j. Thomas Long Esqr Died May the j9th, j730, aged 73.

Near this place lyeth the body of Anna Maria, wife of Samuel Twyford, who departed this life November j9th, Anno Dom. j7jj, aged 22 years. Near this place also lyeth the Body of Anna Maria, daughter of Samuel Twyford, aged 2 months.

Neare vnto this stone Lieth the body of Ivdeth Snell, late wife of Richard Snell of Loxwell, gent: eldest daughter of William Baylyffe of Movnton, Esq., whoe departed this life the third of December Aº Dmi, 1628.

Neare vnto this Place lyeth interred the Bodie of Anne, the davghter of Samvel Twiford of this Bvrrovgh Gent., who was baptized the 13th day of December, Aº. 1672, and departed this life the 16th day of Ivne, Aº 1674.

Neare this Stone lies enterred the Body of Elizabeth Bayliffe, one of the Daughters of Edward Goddard, late of Hartham, Gent, & late Wife of William Bayliffe, now of Movnckton, Gentleman, who departed this life Nov. 3rd, 1652.

Neare this place is buried the Body of Elizabeth, the daughter of Mr Samuel Twyford, who was baptized the 8th day of August, Anno Dom, 1681, and departed this life the 20th day of Ianuary then next following.

Near this place lieth the body of Anne, ye wife of Roger Warne, who died Ivne ye 24th, A.D. 1724, aged 69 years. Allso the body of Roger Warne, who died Decbr the 26, A.D. 1780, aged 80 years. Also the body of Dorcas, ye davgr, who died May the 1st, 1731, aged 35 years.

P.M.S. juxta depositum jacet Quod mortale fuit Johannis Holland, Hujus Parochiæ, Arm., Qui ob. 25ti Aprilis, Anno Salutis 1728, Ætatis 52. Animam Deo reddidit, Corpus Sepulchro, et Famam Posteris. [Dorothie, ux. ej. ob. 3º Aprilis, 1726, Æt. ... Roger Holland, filius, hujus Parochiæ, arm. ob. Julii 8, Æt sexag., 1762].

Near vnto this place lieth inter'd the bodies of Mr Jonathan Giare the late Vicar of this place and his two sons which said Vicar departed this life the 26th day of December in the yeare of ovr Lord 1680.

> Stars fall, bvt in the grossnesse of ovr sight
> A good man dying, the world doth lose a light;
> While we lament ovr loss svch lights pvt ovt,
> The heavens triumph, above the angels shovte.
> If vertve itselfe with vertvovs men covld dy,
> Reader thov then mighst say here doth it ly.

Hic jacent Ossa Viri desideratissimi Johannis Merewether, M.B.,—Ædis Christi apud Oxonienses olim Commensalis, Obiit Maii 24. Anno Domini 1774, Ætatis suæ 88. Hic jacet Maria Uxor Johannis Merewether,

M.B., Obiit Julii 12, Anno Domini 1756, Ætatis suæ 50. Hic etiam sepulta est Anna, Prædicti Johannis Merewether filia, Ob. 11 die Martis, 1823, Anno Ætatis suæ 85. Hic etiam sepulta est Eleanor, Prædicti Johannis Merewether filia, Obt 17mo die Septembris 1831, Anno Ætatis 89.

Near this place Lyeth the Body of the Rev. Mr. Robert Cock, Vicar of this Parish, who by Will left for ever the yearly Produce of Fifty Pounds (which was all he had) for Teaching Poor Girls to Read and Instructing them in the Knowledge and Practice of the Christian Religion as Profess'd and Taught in the Church of England. He Dy'd Oct: 4th Anno Dom: 1724, Ætat: 57.

In memory of William Heaven Wicks who died April 22nd, 1838, aged 54 years. Also of Mary Parkin Wilson, the beloved wife of John Wilson, M.A. and only child of Joanna and the above William Heaven Wicks, who died October 25th, 1848, aged 23 years and 4 months. And lastly of Joanna, wife of the above William H. Wicks, who died June 7th, 1868, aged 84 years.

A painted window—SS. Matthew and Andrew, and various angels Visiting the sick—clothing the naked—feeding the hungry—entertaining the stranger.—To the glory of God and in loving memory of Broome Pinniger and Martha his wife who fell asleep, the former on June 10th, 1875, the latter on March 27th, 1870 This memorial window is placed by their eldest daughter and only son in this church where their Parents worshipped together for nearly 50 years. 1882.

In memory of Gabriel Goldney Esqr, of this parish, who died the 3rd of August 1790, aged 58 years. Also of Thomas Goldney Esqr brother of the above who died the 28th of October 1797, aged 60 years. Also of Sarah relict of the above Gabriel Goldney who died the 29th of January 1814 aged 78 years.

In a vault underneath are deposited the remains of Esmead Edridge Esqr, of Monkton juxta Chippenham, who died March 12th 1812, aged 64 years. And of Catherina Elizabetha, his widow, who died Febry 13th, 1826, aged 78 years. Also of Thomas Edridge Esqr who died April 23rd 1830, aged 81 years. Also of Edward Michell Esqr who died Decr 17th 1834 in his 58th year. Also of Anne Michell who died June 19th 1844, aged 60 years. Also of Graham Francis Moore Michell Esmeade Esqr who died at Cobham, Surrey, 8th October 1883, aged 77 years.

Isabella Maria Constantia Edridge, Wife of Abraham Lloyd Edridge, of Pockeredge in the County of Wilts, died March 28th, 1820, aged 44 years

In Memory of Henry Singer Esqre who died October 18th, 1778, aged 70 years, of Richard Singer Esqre, his Son, who died April 27th, 1802, aged 63 years, and of Harriet, Daughter of the above named Richard Singer by Maria Parry his Wife, who died October 30th, 1790, aged 7 Years. Their Remains are deposited in the Chancel of this Church. Also in Memory of Richard

Oriel Singer Esquire, late of his Majesty's 32nd Regt, only Son of the said Richard Singer by Maria Parry his Wife, who died October 15th, 1818, aged 37 Years. His Remains are deposited at North Wraxall in this County. Also in Memory of Maria Parry Singer, Relict of the above Richard Singer Esquire, who died 26th of April, 1823, aged 76 years. Her remains are deposited at North Wraxall.

To the Memory of John Gould Heath, an Ensign in the Dorset Regiment of Militia, son of John Heath of this Place, Gentleman. He died suddenly at Ivy Bridge Inn in the County of Devon, and was interred in the Church-Yard of Harford in which Parish the Inn is situated. Obiit 7th of June, 1810: Æt: 24 years. Also to the Memory of the above named John Heath, Gentleman, who died the 1st day of November, 1814, aged 53 years. Also Ann, widow of John Heath, who died January 22nd, 1827, aged 63 years.

In memory of William Gundry, Esq who died March 4, A.D. 1853, aged 7....years. Also of Ruth, his wife, who died May 4, A.D. 1855, aged 52 years. Their remains are deposited in Backwell church, Somersetshire.

In memory of Mr William Poole, for many years treasurer of this Borough, who departed this life June 7, A.D. 1850, aged 69 years. His remains are interred at Newton St Loe in the County of Somerset. To certify to the many virtues which characterized his exemplary and useful life this tablet is erected by his friends and fellow townsmen.

In the next alley over against this stone lieth the body of Thomas Batten of Allington who departed this life the 26th of December A⁰ Dmi 1628.

Neare this place lyeth the body of John Ely gent. sometimes bvrgesse of the town who died Novem. 2nd 1663.

> Tis well I am stone to preserve his name
> Who was (if mortalls may be) withovt blame;
> In his religeovs civil practise ivst,
> In his calling no traytour to his trvst;
> If this report consvming time shall weare
> And wipe ovt, search heaven's records tis there.

Neare to this place lyeth also the body of Mary relict of John Ely gent who died Oct the 19th 1671.

> The tablet of my life was black and white,
> Some clovdy dayes I lived to see some bright,
> Bvt now there is no mixtvre all is cleare,
> Tis perfect sunshine I am with my deare,
> Of whom the world was not worthy nor I,
> Happy once more in his blest company.

Nere this place lyeth the body of Richard son of John Ely gent. who died the 2jst of Jvly A⁰ Dm. j676 aged 23 yeares.

> Though death would not upon his head
> The almond tree permit to grow,
> Yet shall the vertues of the dead
> In dust and ashes bud and blow.

Neere this place lieth the body of Marye Pinching the wife of Robert Pinching who dyed the 12th daye of Febrvarye A⁰ Dⁱ j643. Here also lyeth ye body of May ye son of Robert & Mary Pinching who departed this life ye 5th day of October j696 aged 70 yeares.

Near this place lyeth the body of Elinor the wife of May Pinchin who departed this life ye sixteenth day of February in ye year of ovr Lord j7jj aged 68 years.

Here lyes ye body of George Scott, Clothier, who departed this life Aug ye 24 A° D : j698 ætat: Suæ 44.

Neare this place lys interr'd ye body of John Scott gent, son of Mr John Scott Clothier who departed this life the 4th day of April Ano Dom 1700 ætatis. ....

The body of Walter Scott gen. late one of Bvrgesses of this Bvrrovgh who died ye ffifteenth of March Anno Dom. j7$\frac{14}{15}$ Ætatis svæ 55.

John Scott, gent. son of John Scott, Clothier, 4 Aprill 1700 ætatis suæ—Prov. xiv. 32.

> Remember what
>   The wise man saith
> The Righteous
>   Hath hope in death.

George Scott Clothier Aug 24 1689 æt. suæ 44

> Trust not vain man in health or strength
>   Or any worldly store
> For stript and naked you must goe
>   Where I am gone before.
> But trust in GOD and keep His laws
>   And then lay blame on me
> When you come here into the grave
>   If Death part GOD & thee.

Neare this place lieth the body of Alice the wife of Henry Govldney Clothier and the davghter of Mr Richard Scott who was interred the 4th day of Aprill 1670 and was baptized the 11th of October 1638.

Mary, wife of Thomas Chappell of this Burrough Clothier, & daur of Mr Thos Andrews minister of GOD'S Word at Shaston Co Dorset 15 Feb 1639

> Noe sooner are we borne to live then dy
> Our first day doth assure us of our last
> Whilst every moment we doe hasten nigh

> To our long home & what w'have lived is past.
> For man to live here ever cannot be
> Long to enjoy wee must not think, a change
> Attends us, and thou groneing waitst to see
> That day, dear soule, life here at last seemed strange
> Twas sickness, now thou livst when death hath wrought
> Its malice and soe ended hath all greif
> Happy be those mishaps wh thee have brought
> A gaineful loss & in thy death a life.

A large monument with two brass plates.

First brassplate. The Memoriall of Sr Gilbart Pryn, Kt, who married Mary the eldest davghr of Iayne Davys, davghr to Sr Wymond Carye, Kt, Lord Warden of ye Stanneries, Mr of ye First Frvits Office, & Kt of ye Bathe, the said Sr Gilbrt Pryn having issve by ye said Mary his wife seaven children 2 sonnes & 5 davghrs, five of wch 2 sonnes & 3 davgrs are dead; the other 2 daughrs namely ye eldest of all Fravnces is married to Sr Francys Seimovr, Kt, yovngest sonne of ye Lord Beavchamp, sonne & heire to ye now Erle of Hertford, & ye second davghr named Seimovr married to Sr George Hastings, Kt, second brother to Henry now Erle of Hvntingdon. He was buryed June 21, j627.

Second brassplate. *A man in armour—a tree—a woman, in costume of period, holding a bough.*

> Eche man's a plant: and every tree
> Like man, is svbiect to mortalitie.

Five boughs lying down in a row.

> These bravnches dead and fallen away are gone
> From vs vntill the Resurrection.

A man in armour and a woman in costume of the period either side of a graft, each touching a bough—the same repeated.

>These grafted thvs by wedlock's sacred dome,
>(GOD gravnte) may flovrishe till those other come.
>Erected 1628.
>She the 20 Jan. j628

A painted window—Annunciation—Visitation—Birth of our Lord—Adoration of the Magi and various saints and angels.—

To the glory of GOD and in memory of James Utterson, who fell asleep June 27th 1884 in the 80th year of his age; this window is given by his widow Elizabeth Utterson.

In the vault underneath are deposited the remains of James Norris, Esqr.,—(son of the late William Norris Esqr.) of Nonsuch House in this County who departed this life January 3rd, 1835, aged 65 years.

Sacred to the memory of Elizabeth Norris, Relict of the late William Norris, Esq, of Nonsuch House, Wilts, who died May 20, 1805, aged 75. Also to the memory of Elizabeth Norris, Daughter of the above Elizabeth Norris, who died March 17th, 1805 aged 56.

In the vault underneath this spot are deposited the remains of Dyonisia Norris who died on the 25th of June, 1832. And also of Mary Ann Norris who died on the 15th of July 1834, daughter of the late William Norris Esqr of Nonsuch House in this County.

Near this Place Lyeth the Body of Thomas, Figgins Junr., Gent. who departed this life the 9th day of August, 1757, aged 28 years. Also Jane the wife of Thomas Figgins Senr, Gent. died the 20th day of March, 1767, aged 82 years. And also the Body of Thomas

Figgins Senior, Gent. who died the 11th day of August, 1777, aged 74 years. Also Susanna Merewether, Wife of Thomas Figgins, Junr, Gent, and Relict of John Merewether, Gent. died 27th August, 1807, aged 75 Years. Also Ann Figgins, Wife of John Figgins, Gent: died May 7th, 1837, aged 78 Years. Also John Figgins, Gent: died September 19th, 1830, aged 82 years.

A painted window—the fourteen Apostles—Samuel brought to Eli—Christ in the midst of the Doctors—working in the carpenter's shop—little children brought to Christ.—
To the glory of God and in memory of William Lewis who died Ianvary 11 1866 aged 36 years and of William Hall Lewis his only child who died Avgvst 17, 1868, aged 13 years; this window is given by Elizabeth Lewis widow and mother of the above.

This monument is erected to the memory of James Bracher Burnett, third son of Henry Burnett Esqr and Mary his wife, born March the 31st, 1794, and died July the 19th 1840 aged 46 years. Also of Henry Jones Burnet, eldest son of the above Henry and Mary Burnet, who died the 24th March 1795, aged 5 years and 4 months.

Sacred to the memory of Mary, the wife of Ralph Hale Gaby Esqr who departed this life Janry 6th, 1814, aged 69 years. Also of Ralph Hale Gaby Esqr who died December 16th, 1829, aged 80 years.

Near this Place lye Interr'd the Bodies of Anthony Martyn, Gent., who died on the j9th Day of March j7j9 in the 6jst Year of his Age. His Wife Mary

Martyn expired the j7th of April j73j aged 70 Years.
*Robert Martyn—of the Inner Temple Esqr their only Son—died the j2th of August j733 in the forty-fourth Year of his Age.

* On the floor a stone to him and his widow Mildred Holland.

XV. WEST TYTHERTON.

THIS Chapelry is so called to distinguish it from East Tytherton in the parish of Bremhill: it bears also the names of Tytherton *Lucas* (from a family in possession in 1202), Titherington (Aubrey), and more anciently Tudrington and Tet-kirton. This is perhaps the Titherington in which Two Hides of land were held at the Norman Survey by " Borel," to whom belonged the neighbouring Manor of Langley, from which it is separated by the Avon.* In 1352 Sir John Delamere (then of Langley and Leigh) had lands here. Bradenstoke Abbey possessed some lands, which at the Dissolution were granted to H. Goldney. Aubrey says of Tytherton——" *It hath been a good while in possession of Stokes and Barrett, in partition.*" On the garden wall of the old Manor House the shield of Barrett is still to be seen; and on a tablet in the Church the name—— " Hugo Barrett, who slept in the LORD, June 22, 1627, *æt.* 84." William Barrett, born 1735, the Historian of Bristol, belonged to a family in or near Chippenham. Over the door of the Manor House is a handsome stone shield, dated 1702, bearing the arms of Andrews and

* A large portion of Tytherton was in Langley Burrell until lately absorbed into Chippenham parish.

Townsend.   Of the Stokes family there are these inscriptions in the Church——

Here underneath lieth the body of Mrs. Alice Jacob, late wife of Thomas Jacob, of Wootton Bassett, gent, who changed this mortal for an immortal life, the last of Febr. 1653, and left issue John Jacob, of Norton, gent, Sibbilla the wief of Newell Maskeline of Purton, gent, and Elizabeth the wife of Edward Stokes, of this parish, Esq.

Underneath this place lyeth the body of Edward Stokes, Esq. who departed this life in the faith our LORD JESUS CHRIST, the 31 day of Oct. in the 56th year of his age, A.D. 1667.

There are also tablets to the memory of the families of Crook, Uncles, Bayliffe, Wood, and others.

Aubrey writes——" Anno Domini 1652, was printed a booke, called 'The Wiltshire Rant,' being A Narrative of the most unparelleled Prophane Actings, Counterfeit Repentings, and Evil Speakings of Thomas Webbe, late pretended Minister of Langley Buriall, by Edward Stokes, of Titherton Lucas, Esq."

Edward Stokes, the writer of this book, was of a family holding property in Langley Burrell, Kington St. Michael, and Tytherton.   To use his own words——

" About the year 1649, one Thomas Webbe came as an Angel of light into these parts, with a great forme of Godliness, in sheep's cloathing; furnished with cunning and expression he ronls up and down till at last he takes up his rest at Langley Burrell, and having obtained the parsonage there he preached and practised, as a conscientious man."

He was patronized by Mrs. Mary White, then resident in the Manor House of Langley Burrell, and scenes of a most scandalous kind having been some time enacted, informations were laid against them before Edward Stokes, of Tytherton, and William Shute, of Chippenham, by whom they were committed to Salisbury gaol. The Jury, *"being for life or death"* acquitted them. Webbe was summoned before the Commission in London, and ejected from the Parsonage of Langley. In vindication of himself and other magistrates, Edward Stokes wrote " *The Wiltshire Rant.*"

" The Church here is a Chapell of ease to Chippenham. In it I find nothing of antiquity." *Aubrey.*

The Church is dedicated to St. Nicholas, and the tithes of the parish of Tytherton were granted by the Empress Maud to Monkton Farley Priory, A.D. 1150. The story has been told (page 147) when and why they became annexed to Chippenham.

EXTRACTS FROM A MEMORANDUM BOOK,

Kept by Thomas Gardiner, of Titherton,

In the years 1661———1724.

A.D.
1679   The great Kittell pot bought the 16th of August cost just £01 06s. 00d.

1682   Bought a green seet rouge at the Vize Green fair that cost just £1 . 3 . 0

1691   Bought a Citell A brass frying pan and A chafing dish About Mickelmas

1680   A Rate made for the disbanding of the Army 3 months pay £3 . 5 . 6

1686½ The great And mighty prodigious Wind was uppon the 18th day of February being the Tuesday the exterordinary great Voilence of it held from 6 of the clock in the morning till after 9*

1690   Richard Bayle of Standley went to Abram Stoakes, Esqr and made an even Account with him from the beginning of the World to that day

1681   Two most strang unwonted seasones of weather the first of Drith the second of rain the month of Apriell May & June till the 20th day Afforded noo raine of Any consarnment at all which brought soo great A scarsity of gras that Cattell was lickt to bee starved but then after the raine came with thunder stormes And showerery weather Abunddant which brought at the later part of the yeare A verey greate store of grase and all the winter after till the Month of March continued with A most Abundance of rayne and very tempesteouse windes

---

* "Anno 1660, I being then at dinner with Mr. Stokes at Titherton, news was brought in to us that a whirlwind had carried some of the haycocks over the high elms by the house. A kinsman of ours, being a little child, was sett on a haycock, and a whirlwind took him up, with half the haycock, and carried him over high elms, and laid him down safe without any hurt in the next ground."

1682   From 15th of Apriell to the 15th May the raine was soo dreadfull that if GOD in His mersey had not withhelld it At that time when it was it appeared lickly to destroy amost All the Lent crop which A great part thereof was much impoverished There have been no such rain by the dayes of Any of this generation nor I suppose in lat ages beefor us And I pray GOD that never noo such Rain may com Again neither by this Ages nor Ages to com which the LORD our GOD According to the rishes of His mersy grant Untoo us   Amen

1687   Sep 5 then bargained with Henry Baynton Esq for the Reversun of the Widdow Harpers House and Close at the prise of 23 pound And a broad pese of owld gould which broad pese of gould was gave in earnese

1698   May 3 it snowed exceeding hard with very great blosumes

Spipak house (1)
bowdown house (2)
hartom house (3)
Esqier aishes house (4)
Corsham house (5)
Dracott house (6)
Cadnum house (7)
bremhill house (8)
Sir Allundo bridgman's house (9)
Esqier hungefords house (10)

1704   All voyd att preassent there is noe geentell man nor woman lives in all theese housses. being writen the 14th day of may 1704

1711   From 21 Dec till 21 March but little frost and veary Little snow nor raine enough in all that time att one time to weatt thorow A good coate then at night a wonderful brave raine   Then it broake up brave weather

(1) Spye Park.   (2) Bowden Hill House.   (3) Hartham Park.   (4) Langley Burrell Manor House.   (5) Corsham Court.   (6) Draycot Park.   (7) Cadenham House, Bremhill, belonging to the Hungerfords.   (8) There was no mansion at Bremhill; it may be Studley House, near Calne, another seat of the Hungerfords.   (9) Bowood Park, the seat of Sir Orlando Bridgeman.   (10) Probably Rowden House, which, however, had in 1704, passed away from the Hungerfords.

XVI. ST. PAUL'S CHURCH,

Langley Burrell.

IN 1852 Chippenham contained a population of 5000 inhabitants, with Church accommodation for 1000 people only, and the population was increasing rapidly in the northern quarter of the town, which is locally situated in the parish of Langley Burrell. The parish Church of Langley Burrell, St. Peter's, which was a mile distant, could receive a congregation only of 170; and the Churchyard was very small. It was therefore proposed to build a Chapel of Ease in Langley Burrell, near to Chippenham, and to form an ecclesiastical district out of the parishes of Chippenham, Langley Burrell, and Hardenhuish. The Ecclesiastical Commissioners sanctioned the transfer of an acre of the Glebe Land of Langley Burrell for the site of the Church and Burial ground; and also of the severance of £50 a year from the Rectorial Tithe of the old parish for initial endowment. A further sum of £1200 for endowment was raised by subscription. The architect of the Church was G. G. Scott; the cost (exclusive of the tower and steeple) was £4000. It was consecrated on Ap. 15, 1854, under the title of St. Paul's

Church, when the Sermon was preached by the Rev. J. E. Jackson, Rector of Leighdelamere and Rural Dean, who remarked that no new Church had been built in that immediate neighbourhood for 700 years.

The advowson is vested in the Bishop of the Diocese, who nominated the Rev. T. A. Strong as first Incumbent.

In 1866 the Perpetual Curacy was constituted a Rectory, being endowed with rectorial tithe.

XVII. CELTIC and SAXON WORDS and EXPRESSIONS

in use in the Parish of Chippenham, and in the neighbouring Villages.

Tishshom	to sneeze
Gammuts	frolics
Wopping	big
Bavins	rough faggots
Contraption	contrivance
Birl } Chimp } Chism }	to break off sprouts from potatoes
Wayjolt	a seesaw
Jiffy	an instant
Flitters	rags, tatters
Limb	a naughty child
Ragamuffin	a rascal
Froar	frozen
Dap	to rebound
Spreethed	rendered sore by cold
Kex	dry stems of plants
Lissom	pliant
Ramshackle	loose, disjointed

Whippersnapper	*a little active man*
Snarl, Snorral	*a tangle*
Taut	*tight*
Mummucks	*small pieces*
Crock	*a metal or earthen pot*
Shramd	*perished with cold*
Lack a daisical	*fanciful*
Rafty	*brown and strong, as bacon*
Haggle	*to hack*
Daddicky	*decayed, as wood*
Dough fig, Lam fig	*Turkey fig*
Heave	*to sweat, as pennant stone; to lift*
Jibbets	*small pieces*
Leaze	*to glean*
Dudder	*to deafen with noise*
Evvet	*an eft, a lizard*
Gaucum	*a simpleton*
Drouth	*dryness*
Slat	*to split*
Dumbledor	*the humble bee; a dunce*
Hoity toity	*conceited*
Gumption	*common sense*
Harum scarum	*wild*
Slippity sloppity	*slovenly*
Proper (prupper)	*true, real, comely*
Peth	*crumb of a loaf*
Rames	*a skeleton*

Diddle	*to deceive*
Suant	*even, easy, gentle*
Ropy	*applied to stringy, unwholesome bread*
Dunch	*dull, stupid*
Heft	*weight*
Ninnyhammer	*a simpleton*
Humdrum	*nonsensical*
Flush	*fledged, as young birds*
Fractious	*fretful, disobedient*
Teazy	*ill tempered*
Trounce	*to beat*
Froom	*fresh and luxuriant in growth*
Fusty	*musty*
Guzzle	*a sink*
Humbug	*nonsense*
Hullaballoo	*an uproar*
Coom, combe	*a valley*
Casalty	*changeable, as a casalty day*
Huckamuck	*a muddle*
Hudmedud	*a scare crow*
Humpty dumpty	*a dwarf*
Heel	*to turn over*
Nog	*a lump*
Caffy cottrel	*a simpleton*
Harral	*a tangle*
Squat	*to sit on the feet, a bruise*
Leer	*empty and hungry*
Dub	*to pelt*
Basting	*a beating*

Twit	to tell tales upon, to remind of a fault
Bloom	to come over in heat
Blow	to blossom
Caddle / Kiddle caddle	a mess, confusion
Caddlesome	troublesome
Swath	a scythe fall of grass
Bran-new	quite new
Swop	to exchange
Cats cradle	a game with string
Cree	a cry of boys to cease play
Chap	a young fellow, a comrade
Limp	flaccid
With	a faggot band
Quilp	to glutch
Clout	a smack
Ellum	straw for thatch
Fen	to check action at play
Kez	because
Stowls	lower stem and roots of a tree
Mars / Mores	roots of a tree
Quickset (quick)	thorns for hedge
Brize	to bear heavily
Piert	bright and sharp; saucy
Tiert	sharp and painful
Want	a mole
Fall	the autumn
Fess	angry
Ground	a field

CELTIC & SAXON WORDS & EXPRESSIONS 199

Backfriends } Backfringe }	bits of loose skin at the back of fingers
Bannut	dry stems of plants
Flump	a heavy fall
Aneust	almost
Comical } Rum }	curious
In a miconomy	in low spirits
Hasp	the fastening of a door
Rawny	bony
Rumple	to ruffle into folds
Mop	a hiring fair
Mothery	mouldy
Scrunch	to crush
Maunder	to mouth at, abuse
Lief	willing, as, I'd lief go as stay
Leaze	a right of pasture
Sarsen	large stones on the downs
Barken	a small farm yard
Becall	to abuse
Charm	confused sounds
Blubber	to cry, to sob
Ballirag	to abuse
Croopy down	to stoop, as children do
Goodies	sweets, &c.
Grains	malt after infusion
Bams	rough leggings
Happer down	to fall heavily, as rain
Lipping	showery

Lug	a pole, 5½ yards
Chore, char	to go out to work
Gogmire	a quagmire
Lummakin	heavy and idle
Maggots	tricks
Gallivanting	going a gadding
Hulluckye	look here!
Goggles	spectacles
Mazzard	the head
A dot and a don	change of clothes
Main	very
Marly	streaked with fat and lean
Flitmegig	a wild girl
Drock	a drain
Dribs and Drabs	bits
Dead year	year after death
Cham	to chew
Fettle	condition, as, That ground is in good fettle
Halm	stem of plant
Orra one	any
Norra one	none
Rastle	to spread, extend
Plum	soft and yielding, as India rubber
Rumpus	a row
Shard	a breach in a hedge
Skag	a tear in linen, &c
Smeech	a dust
Slomakin	sluttish
Tallet	a hay loft

Stodge	. .	*thick liquid*
Neddy	. .	*a donkey*
Stout	. .	*a gad fly*
Tussle	. .	*a struggle*
Taffy noodle	. .	*a simpleton*
Cockrel	. .	*a young cock*
Tisty tosty	. .	*a cowslip ball*
Unkid	. .	*dismal, dreary*
Voreright	. .	*rude, candid*
Quist	. .	*a wood pigeon*
Wallop	. .	*to beat*
Sprack	. .	*lively*
Scrubby	. .	*inferior, mean*
Dowse	. .	*a slap on the mouth*
Bissom	. .	*a broom*
Wivel	. .	*to veer about, as wind*
Blossoms	. .	*snow flakes*
Gee	. .	*to encourage horses to go, also v.n. to agree, as they do'nt gee well together*
Hallege	. .	*a heap of rubbish*
Loo	. .	*in the shelter*
Mooch	. .	*to play truant*
Durns	. .	*sides of a doorway*
Fantag	. .	*fuss*
Trumpery	. .	*rubbish*
Gawkum Ninkum }	. .	*a booby*
Fluster	. .	*to bustle*
Fiz	. .	*to hiss, as hot iron in water*

Frizzle	*to toast meat*
Rapscallion	*a rascal*
Trim-tram	*a turnstile*
Trit-trot } Trapse }	*to tramp*
Flop	*thick liquid*
Whist	*wretched*
Quandary	*a dilemma*

The Vicar of Kington St. Michael's and his Lumbago.

Ye Vicker o' Kineton, he wun day cum'd drippin' home;
Catch'd a cowld; and afore he wur well, walk'd to Chippinhum.
  Next marnin' a fownd as ad got thik "Lumbago;"
  And wur in for a course o' "Rice puddin and sago."
    To he's Mother a zed,
    "I'll zurely be ded,
  Onless to my Duty at Kineton I may go."
    He's Mother, zed she,
    "Thee be best where thee be,
  Kez thee knowest our Blankets baint bad uns;
    But i' thee wul't be waalking,
    'Taint no yuse I taalking,
  So, I'll e'en set thee down 'mong they mad uns;
  Thee wants to get whoam for Good Friday,
  Kez it be (what I knew'd afore thee did) a High Day:
    Well: ther's Canon Jackson,
    As zound as a Zaxon;
    And ther's Mister Dannel
    As true as a spannel—
      Thee has only to zay
      To ar wun o' they:—
      A Friend in need
      Be a Friend in deed"

J. E. J.

ASH WEDNESDAY SPORTS.

Zays I to my woife, "Mary, I thinks I shall go to Draycut Staple Races. Naashunal spoorts mus' be kip up."

Zays her, "Now do'ant 'e, Giles. 'Tis Ash Wensday, and there's zarvice in Church; now ye woant, will 'e?" zays she, quoite meekloike and tinder; vor my Mary is a voreright Christurn 'ooman, nor a bit o' apocrisy in she.

Zays I, "Mary: Naashunal spoorts mus' be kip up; and a passil of bettermaust vaulks, matter of vourteen dookes, hurls, and mimbers of Parliment, 'a gid in their names, and a' vixed the day."

"'Tis down right hindacent," zays her, main sharp; "zhure, times be bad enuff without our betters makin' mock at relijshun, and a braking the Church rules: 'tis no moor nar a hathan 'ood do."

Zays I, "Mary, Naashunal spoorts mus' be kip up; and maybe the Stooards didnt knaw as how twer Ash Wensday."

"I doant want to argify," her zays, "but why did'nt um look in t' almanac? Bezide thay tells I as how all the passons round writ 'um up a letter (and zo thay ought) and a main strong un too (and zarved 'um roight) and tould 'um as how 'twer jist about a wrong thing to do; t'wer zettin' a bad example to the coontry, and 'ood do a zoite o' mischif, bringin' a zoite of wondermints into a place that niver zeed the loike of it avore. And I heerd too as how the Joostices at Chipnam a Thoorsday last zed as how 'twer a prupper zhame."

Zays I, "Mary, Naashunal spoorts mus' be kip up."

"I tell e what, Giles," hur zed, "they be crool spoorts, and aught niver to be encooraged by noobody. Whoi, eef wun o' them there gintelvauks wer to zee our Jim a' wolloping our neddy, he'd be unmassiful zharp on he, and ha' un off to Vize jale in a jiffy. Hosses be noble hannimals, and tis unmassiful crool to run 'um beyand their strength, a straining the very loife out on 'um, and a birsting ther bleedvessels and a druvving 'um agin stakes and edges, and a braking ther legs, and a putting 'um to despurd haggony, all vor the spoort and amoosement of men, and 'oomen, too."

Zays I, "Mary, Naashunal spoorts mus' be kip up, an' doant matter aboot a bit o' croolty to the poor baste, nar eef a hoss or two is killed, eef us doo git a vew 'ours amoosement out ov' um."

"Oh, Giles!" 'zays Mary, and zhe gied I sich a look that cut I uncummun, it did; and zhe cumd down on I we a bit o' Bible, pat, and zhe zed, zed zhe, "Doant e knaw 'tis writ in the Book—

"A righteous man regardeth the life of his beast?" and then hur calls to our leetle Alice, (a main piert purty leetle maid hur is) and hur zays——"Alice, vetch me the noo radin' book the passon gied e, and rade to vather the vasses you raded to y^r Mother last Zoonday."

Zo Alice vaught the book, and raded to I, just about purty hur did——

> " A man of kindness to his beast is kind,
> But brutal actions show a brutal mind.
> Remember He who made thee, made the brute;
> Who gave thee speech and reason, formed him mute.
> He can't complain—but GOD's all-seeing Eye
> Beholds thy cruelty: He hears his cry.
> He was ordained thy servant, not thy drudge—
> And know that his Creator is thy Judge."

It made I wince, it did; and I veeld very queer and uncoomfortible loike; and Alice zed, " Now doant e go to Races, vather;" and hur lookt so whist and unkid that I wuz main duddered, and wuz aneust a moind to stay at whoame, and goe to Church wi' they—but thinks I, Naashunal spoorts mus' be kip up—and zo I zaddled my hoss, and went to Races.

I zeed what I zeed, and I cumd whoame anigh siven o'clock. Missus and Alice wuz at evenin' zarvice. When Mary cumd in, hur zed, quoite gintle loike, and nar a bit unproachful, " Well, Giles, ha e had a 'appy day?"

" Purty well, purty well, Mary," zays I; " noobody killed as I do knaw; but some o' th' hosses wer despurd hurt. Ther wuz a main purty vew of the bettermaust vaulks, and lots o' ladies, a coontenancing the spoorts, and I doo bleeve I zeed a passon a' peepin' thro' the hedge. But I nivir did zet moine eyes in all my loife on such a hallege of blacks and rapscallions as cumd out of Chipnam; ther wuz a dale of wickedness a goin' on; cussin' and swearin' and gamblin' and drinkin' and voightin'; I count Zatan don a main stroke of bizniz there to day."

"And zumbody," zays my missus, a sort o' soighin' sadly, "must gie account to the LORD vor all this sin."

However, I still zays, as how Naashunal spoorts mus' be kip up, an' now sin' I ha' bin to Ash-Wensday spoorts, I got a new idee in my head. I want som un to writ a letter to the gintlevaulks, and put un in purty words, (as I be a bad scollard of meself) and ax um to zot up some uther owld English games—I mane, Prize Voightin', Cock Voightin', Bull Baitin', and Badger Baitin'." I doe call um all vine ould English spoorts: and vor my piart I doant zee nar a bit o' divverence between any ov um—they be all as good as wun anuther—and eef we moight run hosses to death, we moight zot men and bulls and dogs and cocks to voight, eef it doo gie us amoosement.

Now as Good Vriday is cummin' on, and he's a koind of waste day, (but doa'nt e zay a word o' this to my missus, for hur a got a hawful respec' for Good Vriday, and 'twood aneust brake her 'eart) I doe propose to the gintelvaulks that we ha some spoorts on a Good Vriday. I doo count I cood start two chaps out o' our parish, that 'ood 'andle ther fistis main cleverly; and I got a cock or two that 'ud voight main well vor a beginnin'; and a voine bull dog just about fess, that tored a main peece o' vlesh out o' a tramp's thigh t'other day; and my nevvy ha got a unmassiful girt bull; and we got a frend down west that 'ull send I a badger, (vor they doe lay about his grounds in the sun loike kittuns on a karput;) and eef us can get a main vew o' the gintry to soobscribe to the stakes, I doo bleeve our Good Vriday spoorts 'ood be lots more amoosin' than the Ash Wensday uns.

J. J. D.

XVIII DISTINGUISHED NATIVES OF CHIPPENHAM.

NO doubt there have been many eminent persons born in the parish of Chippenham, whose excellencies have been very great, and whose names might have become very famous——

"Perhaps in this neglected spot is laid
  Some heart once pregnant with celestial fire;
Hands that the rod of empire might have swayed,
  Or waked to exstacy the living lyre.
Some village Hampden, that, with dauntless breast,
  The little tyrant of his fields withstood;
Some mute, inglorious Milton here may rest;
  Some Cromwell, guiltless of his country's blood."
                                GRAY'S ELEGY.

But, unfortunately, *(carent vate sacro*)* for want of a faithful historian of Chippenham, we are left in considerable ignorance of the memorable lives and merits of the multitude of the illustrious departed.

JOHN SCOTT, born in Chippenham in 1638, was the son of a grazier. After serving an apprenticeship to a

---

* They had no poet to record their praise,
  And seal their virtues for these latter days.

trade in London, he studied at New Inn Hall, Oxford, and entered into Holy Orders. In 1667 he was presented to the rectory of St. Peter le Poor, London; in 1684 he was collated to a prebend in St. Paul's Cathedral; but declined a bishopric offered by James II., from unwillingness to take the oaths of homage. He vigourously opposed the advance of Romanism under James, and gave strenuous support to the cause of William III., who conferred on him the important rectory of St. Giles in the Field, and made him a Canon of Windsor. Besides sermons and controversial tracts, he published a valuable treatise on the " *The Christian Life: from its beginning to its consummation in glory,*" in two vols, *folio*. He died in 1694, and was buried in his own Church.

LUDOWIC MUGGLETON, born in Chippenham in 1609, of poor though honest parents, was by trade a tailor. He, and a companion, one John Reeve, proclaimed themselves the two witnesses described in the 11th chap. of the Revelation. They found some followers, and the Muggletonians became one of the many sects with which that unhealthy period swarmed. But they were few, and have always continued few.

Muggleton got into favour with Oliver Cromwell, and, a little before his death, prophecied that the Protector would yet perform many wonderful achievements. But Oliver happening to depart this life before he had done anything more remarkable, Muggleton was asked how it was his prophecy had not come true. He answered very warily, and like himself—"*I am sure His Highness would have performed all, if he had lived long enough.*"

He was pilloried and imprisoned, and his profane books were burnt by the hangman.

Lord Macaulay associates Ludowic Muggleton with George Fox. But Ludowic had no sturdier opponents than the Quakers. William Penn wrote of him as a "*False Prophet and Impostor, guilty of ungodly and blasphemous practices;*" and Ludowic returned answer to William Penn, "*Wherein he is proved to be an ignorant spatter-brained Quaker, who knows no more what the true* GOD *is, nor His secret Decrees, than one of his coachhorses doth; nor so much;* he wrote also "*The Looking Glass for George Fox and other Quakers, wherein they may see themselves to be right Devils.*" In 1829 were published "*Divine Songs of the Muggletonians,*" a curious collection of words that "*accompany the howlings of these wretched fanatics.*'

Muggleton died in 1697, aged 88 years. His portrait, singular in its wan and wild expression, is in the Kensington Gallery.

In 1868 died Mr. Joseph Gandar, of Fitzroy Road, Regent's Park, aged 80, "a sincere member of the sect called Muggletonians for upwards of sixty years." There is only one place of worship in London connected with this extraordinary set of religionists, and not three more in the whole of England.

JAMES HEWLETT.—He was the son of the gardener at Monkton, near Chippenham, where he was engaged to assist his father, but as he seized every leisure moment to draw flowers, fruit, small landscapes, and even heraldic shields, upon doors, walls, slates, &c. Mr. Edridge, his master, scolded him for wasting his time, and dismissed him from his service. His is an instance of a man of genius, who, by integrity and energy, pushed through adverse obstacles, and attained honour and independence. He left his widowed mother in the old Langley tollgate in the north of the town of Chippenham, and obtained employment with a coachmaker of Bath, where he had opportunities of painting coats of arms on the panels of carriages. He rose with great rapidity to fame, having developed exquisite skill in painting fruits and flowers; his works adorned the Exhibition of the Royal Academy for many years; one of his paintings was sold for 400 guineas. Having realized a handsome fortune, he left Bath, and settled at Isleworth, on the Thames, where he died in 1836, aged 67 years.

In connection with James Hewlett, may be mentioned ROBERT ELLIOTT, who, though deaf and dumb from birth, became capable of assisting James Hewlett in painting parts of his splendid pieces, and also himself executed pictures in oil of landscapes and animals, &c. of very considerable merit, the sale of which secured him a comfortable livelihood in his old age. He died at 80. There is a good portrait of him by Alfred Provis in the Wilts Archæological Museum at Devizes.

ALFRED PROVIS.—Alfred Provis was born on Feb. 18, 1818, in a house (now called Orwell House) belonging to his father, John Provis, in the northern part of Chippenham.

John Provis, a timber-merchant and builder, possessed of some property, was a man of thought and reading in advance of his age, had a fair library and collection of fossils, and gave lectures, amongst other subjects, on the History of Chippenham. He made 250 drawings to illustrate a variety of schemes for improving the construction of ships; proposed to Government a plan for cutting a vast canal through the county of Kent to prevent the passage of the Forelands, and wrote 1150 quarto sheets to expound his designs; but the Trinity Board looked coldly upon them. He engaged in heavy contracts for works on the Great Western Railway, then in process of construction in the neighbourhood of Chippenham, and became involved in damaging lawsuits.

By the death of his sister Anne, at 12, and his brother Edwin at 17, Alfred was left an only child, and having at school manifested superior skill in the draftsman's art, his father built him a studio in his garden, and put him under a course of tuition in painting in oils. In early life Alfred Provis left Chippenham, and studied in London under John Wood. Except for very short periods, and at long intervals, the rising young painter never visited Chippenham, so that though he died only three years ago, his person was not known, nor is a single painting of this eminent artist to be found in his native town or in the neighbourhood.

Provis revelled in the love of old buildings and objects, and by far the greater number of his works are pictures of old houses and cottages, especially interiors, portions of old abbeys, porches of churches, &c. hoary ruins, and natural objects venerable with the grace of age. His pictures were very small, from $1\frac{1}{2}$ ft. × 2ft. but they were worked up with exquisite care and finish, so that the objects stood out on the canvas as real and living things.

His pictures soon found admission into the Exhibitions of the Royal Academy, Society of British Artists, Portland Gallery, and other Institutions, and for forty years commanded a ready sale, at from 130 to 180 guineas each.

Of Chippenham and the neighbourhood he painted :

Chippenham Market Place

Interiors of Cottage and Doorway at Studley
      ,,   at South Wraxhall Manor House
      ,,   at Chapel Plaster
      ,,   of Kitchen of Farm House at Stanley

Interiors at Lyneham, and many others
Scott's Mill, Tytherton
Doorway of Manor House, Tytherton
Fireplace near Chippenham
Smithy at Lyneham
Old Farm House near Chippenham

Provis exceedingly admired the picturesque position and architectural characteristics of the semi-ruinous Abbey of Bradenstoke—lodged in the village near for long periods, and painted twenty pictures of different portions of that building, within and without.

After his marriage he lived at Ealing, afterwards at Kingston Lisle, where he was long occupied with Berkshire pieces; he painted also in North Wales; but he frequently left England, for many months in the year, and sojourned in Brittany and Normandy, where the grand old Churches and Chateaux, Crosses, Wells, and especially the Cottages of the peasantry, unchanged in their primitive condition and character, furnished an inexhaustible supply of subjects for his pencil; of these he painted a vast number.

His paintings, not actually architectural, included such subjects as these——

"The Gleaner."—"Girl at the Spring."—"Winter." "Summer."—"Boy at Pump."—"A Bretonne selling her hair."—"Breton Devotion."—"'Viens donc'"—"Breton Courtship."—"The Conway Falls."—"Feeding Chicken."—"Repose."—"'Wait Awhile.'"—"The

Orphans."—"Hush."—"Sunday Morning."—"A Welsh Mendicant."—"The Lace Worker."— "Grandmother's Pets."—"The Singers."—"Spring Flowers."—"'Sit up!'"—"Children and Rabbit."—"Blowing Bubbles." "The Bird's Nest."—"The Lesson."—"'It's not for you!'"—"Old Well and Cottage."—"Friends; a Dog and Child Asleep."—"A Woman Reading," and many others.

Some of Provis's paintings are in the north of England, but most of them were purchased by French and American connoisseurs.

He died at Kingston Lisle, near Wantage, Berks, Aug. 10, 1890, aged 72 years. He left unfinished many interesting sketches in the neighbourhood of Chippenham.

   Old House, Seagry
   Porch of Sutton Church
   Old Chest in Corsham Church
   Door of Cottage, Slaughterford
   Shambles, Chippenham
   Porch of Bremhill Church
   Doorway, Great Chalfield
   Cottage, Allington
   Porch of Stanton Church
   Bradenstoke, entrance to
     &c. &c. &c.

XIX. PERSONS OF NOTE

WHO HAVE LIVED in the NEIGHBOURHOOD OF CHIPPENHAM.

GEORGE HERBERT.——It may not be generally known that George Herbert sojourned a year at Dauntesey House. Dauntesey is eight miles from Chippenham, and Herbert must often have passed through the town in his journeys to and fro. Dauntesey Manor belonged to Lord Danvers, Earl of Danby, whose younger brother, Sir John Danvers, had married Herbert's mother.

Isaac Walton writes——

"Lord Danvers lov'd Mr. Herbert much, and allow'd him such an apartment in that house as might best sute Mr. Herbert's accommodation and liking. And in this place, by a spare dyet, declining all perplexing studies, moderate exercise, and cheerful conversation, his health was apparently improved to a great degree of strength."

The front of Dauntesey House has been rebuilt since Herbert's time, but the rooms in the interior of the mansion remain much in the same condition as when he and his wife resided in it. Search has been made over the house, and especially among the books in the Library to ascertain whether any memorial whatever of Herbert survived, but without success.

It is satisfactory to know that the "choice air" of Dauntesey restored his health. Aubrey speaks of his person——

"He was a very fine complexion and consumptive."

Walton says——

"He was of a stature inclining towards tallness; his body was very strait, and so far from being cumbred with too much flesh that he was lean to an extremity."

There was a gentleman living at Dauntesey, an intimate friend of Herbert's, who told Aubrey that——

"Mr. Herbert was a very good hand on the lute, and that he sett his own lyricks, or sacred poems."

Many of the poems of *The Temple* were probably written in Dauntesey House. On the east side of the Earl of Danby's monument of white marble in Dauntesey Church is inscribed

LAUS DEO

Sacred marble, safely keepe
His dust who under thee must sleep,
Untill the graves againe restore
Their dead, and time shall be no more;
Meanewhile, if he which all thinges weares
Doe ruine thee; or if the tears
Are shed for him dissolve thy frame,
Thou art requited: for His fame,
His vertues, and His worth shal be
Another monument for thee. G. HERBERT.

This epitaph on Lord Danby must have been written before the Earl's death. He survived Herbert more than twenty years.

From Dauntesey, after apparently a pleasant sojourn, Herbert took his wife to her old home at Baynton, in Edington parish, near Westbury, whence he had married her; and Aubrey lets him depart with this just and graceful compliment——

"'Tis an honour to the place, to have had the heavenly and ingeniose contemplation of this good man, who was pious even to prophesie."

JOHN AUBREY, F.S.A.——The Parish of Kington St. Michael is to be remembered as having given birth to two writers on the archæology and topography of Wiltshire, JOHN AUBREY and JOHN BRITTON.

John Aubrey was the earliest collector of memoranda relating to the antiquities of Wiltshire. He was the son of Richard Aubrey, and Deborah Lyte, daughter of Isaac Lyte, of Easton Pierse or Piercy, a small manor in the parish of Kington St. Michael, and was born on Sunday Mar. 12, 1625.

"In an ill hour,"

he said (for he was a believer in astrology)

"Saturn directly opposing my ascendant—in my Grandfather's chamber I first drew my breath, very weak and like to dye, and therefore christened that morning before morning prayer."

"1629. I had a grievous ague, I can remember it. This sickness nipt my strength in the bud. Bred ignorant at Eston—eremetical solitude, was very curious. Did ever love to converse with old men as Living Histories; cared not for play."

"Anno 1633. I entered into my Grammar at the Latin School at Yatton Kaynell, in the Church, where the Curate taught the eldest boys Virgil, Ovid, &c.. 1634, afterwards I went to School to Mr. Robert Latimer, a delicate and little person, Rector of Leigh Delamere—a mile—fine walk—who had an easie way of teaching, but memory not tenacious. In my Grandfather's days the manuscripts (from the old Abbeys) flew about like butterflies. The glovers of Malmesbury made great havock of them; and gloves were wrapt up no doubt in many good pieces of antiquity." .

"I was afterwards under several dull ignorant teachers till 12, about which time I was sent to Blandford School, in Dorset, W. Sutton, B.D., who was illnatured. Here I recovered my health, and got my latin and greeke."

"In 1642. Entered at Trinity Coll. Oxon. In 1643 my Father sent for me home in feare: led a sad life in the country where I conversed with none but servants, rustiques, and soldiers."

In 1646 he was admitted into the Inner Temple, but he was an unsettled and unlucky man. His whole inheritance (once £700 a year) was consumed in paying debts and defending lawsuits. He spent much of his time in riding about his native county, in search, sometimes of "Antiq:" and sometimes of a wife. He had some narrow escapes from matrimony—he was "*suitor to Mistress Jane Codrington.*"

Next year he says

"*I saw that incomparable good gentlewoman Mistress M. Wiseman, with whom at first sight I was in love.*"——1656, a strange year to me; several love and law suits."—— "Obiit Domina Kasker Ryves, with whom I was to marry; to my great losse; £2000."—" 1665. Nov 1. I made my first address (in an ill hour) to Joan Sumner. She lived with her brother at Seend. The next year was more unlucky. 1666. All my affairs ran kim kam; treacheries and enmities in abundance against me. 1667. Arrested in Chancery Lane at Mistress Sumner's suit."

He obtained a verdict against the lady for £600 damages, which sum, on a new trial, was reduced to £300. He was now, he sadly says, in as much affliction as a mortal could be; "*but I submitted myselfe to* GOD's *will; wholly cast myselfe on* GOD's *providence. In monte Dei videbitur.*" (In the mount of the LORD it shall be seen. Gen. xxii. 14. The LORD will provide.)

He still pursued his studies in "Antiq:" wrote "Letters and Lives of Eminent Men," "Miscellanies," "Natural History of Wilts," "Description of North Wilts," "History of Surrey," and many fragmentary Essays.

He spent his later years among his literary intimates, and under the roof of his many noble and hospitable friends, to whom he seems to have been ever acceptable, till (in his journey from London to Draycot) he died at Oxford, and was buried in the Churchyard of St. Mary Magdalen, June 7, 1697. The last words he wrote were——"*I now indulge my genius with my friends, and pray for the young angel's rest."* He was 72 years old when he died.

It has been justly and generously said——" *We account Aubrey, despite his love of ghosts and wonderful accidents, among the benefactors of mankind."*

EDINB. REVIEW, Ap. 1860.

WILLIAM LISLE BOWLES——Bowles has been called *" The Father of the Poets of Nature,"* since, of these Poets, he was not only first in time, but his poetry, though inferior to theirs, inspired Coleridge, Southey, Crabbe, and Wordsworth.

He was born Sep. 24, 1762, at King's Sutton, in Northamptonshire, of which parish his father was Vicar, who afterwards became Rector of Uphill, near Weston Super Mare.

William was brought a child to Uphill Parsonage; —in his poem, " Banwell Hill," he recites the remembrance of his passing over Weston Sands on his way to his new home.

> " I was a child when first I heard the sound
>   Of the great sea. 'Twas night, and journeying far,
>   We were belated on our road, 'mid scenes
>   New and unknown——a mother, and her child,
>   Now first in this wide world a wanderer——
>   When as the wheels went slow, and the still night
>   Seemed listening, a low murmur met the ear,
>   Not of the winds :—my mother softly said,
>   " Listen ! it is the sea "——With breathless awe
>   I heard the sound, and closer pressed her hand.

> When first I heard, at night, the distant sound,
> Great Ocean! of thy everlasting voice,
> When the white Parsonage among the trees
> Peeped out, that night I restless passed.   The sea
> Filled all my thoughts; and when slow morning came,
> And the first sunbeam streaked the window-pane,
> I rose unnoticed, and with stealthy pace,
> Straggling along the village green, explored
> Alone my fearful, but advent'rous way;
> When, having turned the hedgerow, I beheld,
> For the first time, thy glorious element,
> Old Ocean!—glittering in the beams of morn.
>   Shivering I stood, and tearful; and e'en now
> I feel the deep impression of that hour,
> As but of yesterday!——"

In 1776 he entered Winchester School on the Wykeham foundation, under Dr. Wharton, and passed out, as Captain of the School, into Trinity College, Oxford. In 1783 he gained the Chancellor's prize for Latin verse. In 1787 he published "*Fourteen Sonnets written chiefly on Picturesque Spots during a Journey.*"
Let him tell his own story—

"Passing through Bath I corrected and wrote out my Sonnets, and took them myself to the late Mr. Cruttwell, and with much hesitation unfolded my message, which was to enquire whether he would give anything for the Sonnets. He at once declined the purchase, and very much doubted, whether the publication would repay the cost of printing, which would come to about five pounds."

It was at last determined that one hundred copies in quarto should be published as a kind of "forlorn hope."

"Half a year afterwards I received a letter from the printer informing me that the hundred copies were all sold; five hundred more were printed, which went off rapidly; then a third edition of seven hundred and fifty."

Coleridge had already borne testimony to the power of Bowles's verse, in (as it seems) the first sonnet he wrote——

> "My heart has thanked thee, Bowles! for those soft
>   strains,
> Whose sadness soothes one like the murmuring
> Of wild bees in the sunny showers of spring—
> And when the mightier throes of mind began,
> And drove me forth, a thought-bewildered man,
> Their mild and manliest melancholy lent
> A mingled charm——
> Bidding a strange mysterious pleasure brood
> Over the wavy and tumultuous mind."

Coleridge spoke of himself as "*withdrawn from perilous error by the genial influence of a style of poetry so tender, yet so manly; so natural and real, and yet so dignified and harmonious;*" and so powerfully did the Sonnets impress him that he copied them out forty times with his own pen, and gave copies to his young friends.

Soon after the third edition of the Sonnets was published, Cruttwell, the Bath printer, wrote to the author to say that two young gentlemen, strangers, (one a particularly handsome and pleasing youth, lately from Westminster School), had called at his office, and spoke in high commendation of the poems. Bowles knew not then who they were, but from one of them he received a visit in his parsonage at Bremhill forty years afterwards—it was ROBERT SOUTHEY.

On many occasions Bowles visited Bath. During an illness he resided at 5 South Parade, and on a restless night he heard the fall of the waters of the Avon, which flows near, and wrote the verses, beginning,

" When I lay musing in my bed alone
And listen to the wintry waterfall——"

But, while at Bath, he chiefly stayed, in later life, at the Castle Inn, then under the management of a venerable landlady, Mrs. Temple, for whom he had a great respect, and whom he always treated with chivalrous courtesy. Crabbe also put up at the Castle. Moore made the White Hart his temporary home.

When the Royal Literary Institution at Bath was opened by Lord Lansdowne, Bowles, Crabbe, and Moore, were present. Lord Lansdowne alluded to Moore as among the literary ornaments, if not of Bath itself, of its precincts. Moore responded, and said of Bowles:——

"His poetry was the first fountain at which I drank the pure freshness of the English language, and learned of what variety of sweetness the music of English verse is capable. From admiration of the poet, I have been promoted into friendship with the man, and I feel it particularly incumbent on me to say that I have found the life and poetry of my friend to be but echoes to each other, the same sweetness and good feeling pervading and modulating both. His native element is that garden of social life which he adorns, and the proper business and delight of his life are sunshine and flowers."

The Sonnets are the best of Bowles's poems. He has no profound imagination——no "*thoughts that breathe, and words that burn*——" but over much of his poetry falls an autumnal moonlight of pure and pensive feeling; his verses are like the bells of Ostend, as he described them——

"They fling their melancholy music wide."

But his poetry, like that of Southey, Coleridge, and Wordsworth, was much more esteemed fifty years ago, than in this day.

Having entered into Holy Orders, he served, for many years, the Curacy of Donhead St. Andrew, Wilts.

In 1804 he was presented to the Vicarage of Bremhill, near Chippenham, Wilts; and in 1828 became a Canon Residentiary of Salisbury.

He was a Magistrate for Wilts, and often sat on the Bench at the Petty Sessions in the Old Town Hall, Chippenham.

For sixty years, from 1798 to the end of his life, he was writing. Besides many poems, long and short, he composed Histories of Bremhill and Lacock Abbey, a Life of Bishop Ken, and a great many other works. It was said of him that——

"—— playful in habit and conversation, unremitting in duty, zealous in the education of children, he was an exemplary instance of the union of Christian graces with the polish of taste and the amenities of literature."

He was extremely fond of music, and had even his sheep bells tuned in thirds and fifths.

As he advanced in years, and the infirmities of old age increased upon him, he grew forgetful and weak in mind, and his oddities and eccentricities are still remembered in the neighbourhood.

He gave Mrs. Moore a Bible as a birthday present; she asked him to write her name in it; he did so, and added "*From the author.*"

"*I never,*" said he, "*had but one watch; and I lost it the first day I wore it.*" Mrs. Bowles whispered—"*And if he got another to-day, he would lose it before night.*"

One day he walked up to a turnpike gate, and presented 2d for the toll, "*What is this for, sir?*" said the keeper. "*For my horse, of course.*" "*But, sir, you have no horse.*" "*Dear me,*" exclaimed the astonished poet—"*am I walking?*"

Many visitors came to the Parsonage at Bremhill, not only to see the beautiful lawns and gardens studded with relics and memorials, but to obtain the honour of speaking to the aged poet and divine. Mrs. Bowles had to keep a watchful eye lest the good old man should rob her Drawing room of all its treasures, as presents to the pilgrims.

When a guest at Bowood (where he was also Chaplain), his bell rang violently one morning, and on the startled valet appearing, the Canon protested that a thief had entered the chamber in the night, and stolen one of his stockings. Search was made in vain, and it was proposed either to borrow a stocking of one of the visitors, or send post haste to Bremhill, when it was discovered that he had put two stockings on one leg.

He was greatly afraid of dogs, and always wore leggings for protection. Visiting at a house in Devizes, a little cur barked at him, when he fled into a room, looked the door, and was found standing on a chair, fervently thanking GOD for his providential deliverance.

While at the Castle and Ball Hotel, Bath, he would often forget the hour at which he had ordered his dinner. He would go out, and on his return, hours after it was ready, would first proceed to the Bar, to pass compliments with Mrs. Temple, when she would say, in her own graceful manner, "*After you have dined, Mr. Bowles, if you please.*" Once he was found at the White Hart Hotel, where he had laid hold on the waiter, to whom he was dictating his conceptions of the True Sublime in Poetry.

Thomas Moore, whom Bowles often visited at Sloperton Cottage, wrote in his Diary towards the end of his life; "*What with his genius, his blunders, his absences, he is the most delightful of all existing persons.*" And Southey remarked of him——"*His oddity, his untidiness, his simplicity, his benevolence, his fears, and his good nature, make him one of the most entertaining and extraordinary characters I ever met with.*"

In extreme old age, he went to Weston Super Mare

once again, and there indited one of the most pathetic of his pieces, and probably the last.——

" Was it but yesterday I heard the roar
Of these white coursing waves, and trod the shore,
A young and playful child—but yesterday?—
Now I return with locks of scattered grey,
And wasted strength—for many, many years
Have passed; some marked by joy, and some
    by tears,
Since last we parted.   As I gaze around
I think of Time's fleet step, that makes no sound.

In yonder vale, beneath the hill-top tower,
My father decked the village Pastor's bower*——
Now he, and all between whose knees I played,
Cold in the narrow cell of Death are laid.
" MY FATHER," to the lonely surge I sigh—
" MY FATHER," the lone surge seems to reply—
Yet the same shells and seaweeds seem to strew
The sandy margin, as when life was new.

I mourn not Time's inevitable tide,
Whose swift career ten thousand feel beside;
I mourn not for the days that are no more;
But come a stranger, Weston, to thy shore
In search of health alone, and woo the breeze
That wanders o'er thy solitary seas;
To chase the mists from these oppressed eyes,
And renovate life's languid energies."

    * Bowles's father planted the grounds at Uphill Parsonage.

He died in the Close, Salisbury, on Ap. 7, 1850, aged 88, and his was the last corpse buried within the walls of the Cathedral.

THOMAS MOORE was born in Ireland, in 1779.* In 1795 he entered Trinity College, Dublin; he had already written some verses, and of these, as of others of very questionable propriety composed in after years, there were many

"Which dying he would wish to blot."

In 1811 he married Bessy Dyke, fourteen years his junior—and through a wedded life of more than forty years he rendered to her a fond and faithful attachment; she was ever his "dear girl," "his darling Bessy"—and Bessy, wholly devoted to the duties of home, returned his love with an ardent affection that knew no bounds. They had five children.

Moore's talent of writing verses in sweetly flowing language† and singing his own songs in a soft, expressive, tenor voice, wedded to new and pathetic melodies, lifted him into the highest walks of fashionable society.

Amongst his most devoted admirers and loyal friends were the Marquis and Marchioness of Lansdowne. At their recommendation he and his Bessy came into Wilt-

---

* The Rev. W. H. Hitchcock, *passim.*

† Bowles gave him a book, and wrote—"*Inter poetas suaves suavissimo*"—*i.e.* "To the sweetest among sweet poets."

shire, and fixed their residence at Sloperton Cottage, a small thatched house, furnished, at a rent of £40 a year, in the parish of Bromham, about three miles from Bowood.

"It was a cottage of gentility, with two gateways, and pretty grounds round it in a delightful country: the poet's study upstairs in which close and hard work was done; and in the garden a raised walk running its whole length, and bounded by a hedge of laurel, the favourite walk of the poet."

Most of the Irish Melodies, the History of Ireland, the Life of Lord Byron, with a multitude of ephemeral papers, were written at Sloperton. Moore composed much in the open air, while walking by the side of the laurel hedge. "There," as he said, "in the country we will live on Love, Literature, and Liberty."

Bowood House was then occupied by Henry, third Marquis of Lansdowne, and thither, through Lord Lansdowne's urbanity and hospitality, converged statesmen, scholars, poets, artists, and divines.

At that time almost all the mansions of the gentry in the neighbourhood were filled with genial families.

There were the Phipps family, then at Wans House; the Starkeys, at Spye Park; the Lockes, of Rowdeford; the Hughes, of Buckhill; the Talbots, of Lacock Abbey; the Moneys, of Whetham; the Taylors, of Erlestoke; the Clutterbucks, of Hardenhuish; the Scropes, of Castle Combe; the Merewethers, of Castlefield; the Awdrys, of

Notton and Seend, with Canon Bowles at Bremhill, and Henry Drury, then Curate of Bromham.

Amongst all these families Moore was a thrice honoured guest—he was admired, flattered, and caressed by all—much for his brilliant, fascinating conversation, more for his unparalleled power in singing—"*that never to be forgotten melodious warbling.*" Ladies and gentlemen were often obliged to leave the room in floods of tears over the Melodies. Once, at Bowood, Moore himself could not refrain from crying as he sang—Bowles cried—the poet Rogers cried—Young, Vicar of Lyneham, cried—and Lord Lansdowne could scarcely prevent himself from being swept away, as he said, by "*the high poetical excitement.*"

There were many good influences around Moore at Bowood, infusing into his poetry a healthier and purer tone, and of these the most benign was that of Louisa Emma, Marchioness of Lansdowne; Moore's constant intercourse with Lady Lansdowne, as Lord John Russell allowed in his Life of Moore, "*led him to revere a woman unspotted from the world, who diffused an air of holiness, and peace, and purity, over the house of Bowood, which neither rich nor poor can ever forget.*"

But though Sloperton Cottage was a home of love and peace, cares and sorrows often broke in. Through no fault of his, Moore became involved in serious pecuniary responsibilities.

But saddest affliction of all, they lost all their children. Barbara died at five years old; Olivia at one year. Anastasia Mary, the youngest girl, reached the age of sixteen: she was her father's pride and joy, his companion in his study, and in his walks; her presence was to him as the presence of an angel; he used to say —"*She is so pure;* GOD *keep her so.*" As they were walking in the garden one day, he sang——

> "Little May Fly,
>   Both you and I
>   Should bless that GOD in heaven,
>   By Whom the flower,
>   The bee, and bower,
>   For our delight were given."

She died in 1829, and was buried in Bromham Churchyard.

John, a young officer of 18, came home from India to die in his mother's arms; Thomas, the eldest, died in Algeria, aged 28. Then the bereaved father made entry in his diary——

"The last of our five children is now gone—and we are left desolate and alone."

Moore was born of a Roman Catholic family, and he was himself professedly a Romanist; but he allowed his children to become members of the English Church, and frequently attended the Services in Westminster Abbey, and in the Domestic Chapel at Bowood, where, he says in his Diary, he often heard Canon Bowles preach.

The loss of his last child not only deeply saddened his heart, but clouded his intellect; he lost his memory, and became semi-childish. The last time he attempted to sing was at Wans, but he could not remember the old familiar words, and said he would never sing again. Before his death he "*warbled*," as his wife expressed it, and said to her "*Trust in* God, *Bessy, trust in* God." He died on Feb. 26, 1852, and was buried beside Anastasia. Mrs. Moore outlived her husband thirteen years, dying on Sep. 4, 1865.

Moore deeply regretted, in later life, the folly and frivolities of his youth, and the coarseness and corruption of his early writings; the latter he made earnest endeavours to recall and purify. On one of his last birthdays he laments——

> "Ah! 'tis not thus the voice that dwells
>   In sober birthdays speaks to me;
> Far otherwise—of time it tells,
>   Lavished unwisely, carelessly—
> Of counsels mocked—of talents, made
>   Haply for high and pure designs,
> But oft, like Israel's incense, laid
>   Upon unholy, earthly shrines."

Howitt, in his "Homes and Haunts of the British Poets," having spoken with some severity on Moore's life, concludes—"yet he was a most affectionate husband, son, and brother—the best part of his character was his affection for his parents, his wife and children; the best part of his genius is to be found in his Irish Melodies and Lalla Rookh."

But go, stand beside the grave of Moore in Bromham churchyard, and remember and repeat his own words——

> "This world is all a fleeting show,
>   For man's illusion given;
> The smiles of joy, the tears of woe,
> Deceitful shine, deceitful flow—
>   THERE'S NOTHING TRUE BUT HEAVEN.
>
> And false the light on Glory's plume,
>   And fading hues of even;
> And Love, and Hope, and Beauty's bloom
> Are blessings gathered from the tomb—
>   THERE'S NOTHING BRIGHT BUT HEAVEN.
>
> Poor wanderers of a stormy day,
>   From wave to wave we 're driven;
> And Fancy's flash, and Reason's ray
> Serve but to light our troubled way—
>   THERE'S NOTHING CALM BUT HEAVEN."*

JOHN BRITTON, F.S.A.——This name was familiar for the past half century to all the archæologists, scholars, and artists of Great Britain, and indeed of Europe, and his life supplies another example of de-

---

* "No longer seek his merits to disclose,
   Nor draw his frailties from their dread abode;
 There they alike in trembling hope repose—
   The bosom of his Father and his GOD."
                              GRAY'S ELEGY.

termination, perseverance, and triumph, over almost unsurmountable difficulties.

John Britton was born in a humble cottage in the village of Kington St. Michael. The house became ruinous and was removed a few years ago; but an inscribed stone in the wall now marks the site—— "JOHN BRITTON, 1771." He was the eldest son of ten children, brought up in a single small room. His father, a baker, maltster, shopkeeper, and farmer, "encumbered with many trades without success in any," sank into poverty.

The mother, a worthy woman, contended bravely against misfortune, bad debts, cheating millers, rivalry in trade, and an overwhelming family, and died of a broken heart. After receiving whatever imperfect education the villages around could afford, John Britton went to School in Chippenham, and afterwards was apprenticed by an uncle to a tavern keeper in London, who set him to work in an underground wine-cellar, a dismal life of ten hours a day, to which Britton always looked back with utter abhorrence. He borrowed and eagerly read whatever books came within his reach; left his dreary servitude before his time, and, poor and sickly, sought help of his two uncles in London, neither of whom would give him a meal. But he yet struggled onwards and upwards, with an indomitable heart, and at length, aided by one friend and another, entered on a literary life of indefatigable industry which extended over sixty years of almost incessant labour.

His first great work was the "BEAUTIES OF WILTSHIRE,"* followed rapidly by other noble books, profusely illustrated at enormous cost, amongst which was "Cathedral Antiquities of England," in fourteen magnificent volumes. On his 74th birthday he was presented with a testimonial, which reached £1000, and this was partly expended in printing his "Autobiography;" on which Southey pertinently remarked,

"The memoirs of a man, who from such circumstances, and under such difficulties, made his way to a station of respectability, is one of the most useful and encouraging lessons that can be placed in the hands of the young."

John Britton died on Jan. 1, 1857, in his 86th year, and was buried in Norwood Cemetery, where a vast unwrought monolith marks his grave.

A painted window, in joint memorial of Aubrey and Britton, was erected in Kington St. Michael Church, by the exertions of Canon Jackson. [A stained-glass

---

* Britton writes that when he first contemplated composing a work on Wiltshire, he was impelled to establish a starting point at CHIPPENHAM, with which town he was best acquainted; but that his spirits sank within him when he found how little was known of its local history. But he adds—"I was tempted to persevere by the encouragement I received from the Rev. Josiah Allport, *(Curate in sole charge of the Parish Church, an eminent evangelical preacher and sound scholar)*, James Coombs, Robert Sadler, and John Provis, all of Chippenham."

All honour to the memory of these men of Chippenham whose sympathy cheered on the brave young Britton (Briton) in the stern battle of life.

window in the same Church would be an appropriate testimonial to the memory of Canon Jackson himself.]

Canon Jackson also wrote a summary of Britton's life, wherein he gives a classified list of his books amounting to 57 volumes, containing 17,254 pages, illustrated by 1867 engravings.

"But *(it has been well said)* what arithmetic can tell us the amount of time, mental and manual labour, care and anxiety, which these productions must have involved? Seldom has public money been more deservedly applied than the pension of £75 a year devoted to this indefatigable and useful writer, in the Chancellorship of Mr. Disraeli."

WILTSHIRE WORTHIES.

JOHN EDWARD JACKSON, F.S.A. Born in Doncaster, Nov. 12, 1805, John Jackson was educated at the Charter-House, where he attained the Captaincy of the School. He matriculated at Brazen-Nose College, Oxford; took a Second Class in *Lit. Human*, B. A. in 1827, M.A. in 1830. In 1834 he was ordained Deacon on the title of Farleigh Hungerford, Somerset, and received Priest's Orders in 1836.

In 1845 he was presented to the Rectory of Leigh Delamere with Sevington by Joseph Neeld, Esq. of Grittleton House, and the next year by the same patron to the Vicarage of Norton, near Malmesbury. He was never married; he said at a Meeting of the Wilts

Archæological Society at Chippenham that "*he often wondered how clergymen could get on in the country villages without a wife*—they did sometimes."

He was nominated by Bishop Monk to an Honorary Canonry in Bristol Cathedral, but he was not a Canon *de facto*, never having been instituted or installed.

As soon as he came into Wiltshire, and found himself surrounded by many objects of congenial interest, he plunged with ardour into the study of the ancient history and antiquities of his adopted county.

Men of Wiltshire have done famous work in collecting and preserving valuable County memoranda, natural, typographical, and historical—such as Bishop Tanner, John Aubrey, Sir R. C. Hoare, Sir Thomas Phillips, and John Britton, but for patient research, critical accuracy, and exhaustive treatment of his subject, on papers purely referring to Wiltshire story, and within the limited area to which he confined himself, Jackson took foremost place.

His chief work, which cost him much time, thought, and labour, and is a monument of severe industry prolonged through many an anxious year, was the heavy quarto——"AUBREY'S and JACKSON'S TOPOGRAPHICAL COLLECTIONS." But it was not worthy of him. It did not become a man of his culture and calibre to sit as a mere annotator at Aubrey's feet. Wiltshire needed a County History, and Jackson could have written it; and if he had concentrated his abilities and the amount of material at his command upon

"THE HISTORY OF WILTSHIRE," he would have left us a legacy worthy of the subject and of the man.

Canon Jackson edited the Wiltshire Archæological Magazine from its commencement in 1853, and contributed to its pages many solid and original papers, in number beyond those of any other writer. Before his connection with the Society he wrote a "History of Grittleton," and of "The Churches of St. Mary and St. George, Doncaster." He was the author of the following compilations, published in the Magazine—

Leland's Journey through Wilts	Stonehenge
Maud Heath's Causeway	Hungerford Chapel
Kingston House, Bradford	Lord Stourton
Chippenham	Rood Ashton
Kington St. Michael	Longleat
Monkton Farley Priory	Wulfhall
Swindon	Amey Robsart
Malmesbury	Sheriffs of Wilts
Vale of Warminster	Selwood Forest
Wraxhall House	Wiltshire Ladies
Ambresbury Monastery	Edington Monastery
Ancient Chapels of Wilts	Cranborne Chase
Heytesbury Alms Houses	Calne
Corsham	Westbury

With many minor treatises.

He died Mar. 6, 1891, in his 86th year, and was buried at Leigh Delamere.

He left several huge folios of unpublished Memorials of the history of the once famous family of the Hungerfords, with Collections of various papers referring to many parishes in North Wilts, and (in larger volume) to the towns of Swindon, Calne, Malmesbury, Chippenham, Warminster, Devizes, Westbury, and others—all these papers, by a note under his own hand, he desired should be entrusted to the Society of Antiquaries, of which he was a Fellow. Just before his death, the Marchioness of Bath, alone, and in inclement weather, came from Longleat to visit her aged friend, and to her he gave two or three large volumes of letters of the Earl of Leicester, and a great many curious documents, *temp.* Queen Elizabeth.

It should be known for the guidance of future Wiltshire bibliographers that the Jackson papers are deposited in the Library of the Society of Antiquaries, Burlington House, London; that they are open to inspection; and that they will be readily lent upon introduction by a F. S. A.

XX. ADDENDA.

Page 3——*Rebus* on the name of Chippenham.

"At a cold entertainment a dish made of pork—
And the tool of a lawyer which ploughs up his lands—
What superfluous remains of a carpenter's work—
 Is the name of a place where my dwelling-house stands. F. B."

ANSWER.

"At a cold entertainment of "Ham" I've oft tasted—
 With the tool of a lawyer a "Pen" will agree—
Of a carpenter's work 'tis a "Chip" that is wasted—
 So you live at "CHIPPENHAM," Master F. B."

GENT. MAG. 1751.

Page 17—For arms of Prynne *quartering* Davys "—read "*impaling.*"

„ 31—For " This spring has flowed "—read, " Was said to have flowed."

„ 40— " Great is the crime in man or woman
To steal a Goose from off the Common—
But what shall be that man's excuse
WHO STEALS THE COMMON FROM THE GOOSE?"

Caroline, Queen of George II., having a design to enclose St. James's Park, and make it into a Garden for the Palace, asked Sir Robert Walpole what it would cost ——"*Madame*," said he, "*I think it would cost your Majesty about Three Crowns.*"

All Commons, Village Greens, Public Paths, and Ancient Ways are now under the protection of the

ADDENDA. 243

Parish Council; it will be the duty of the Parish Council to provide a Cricket Field and Recreation Ground for the use of the parishioners.

Page 47—For "Cloisters of Salisbury Cathedral"—read "Transept." see page 230.

„ 54—For "The Parish of Chippenham include "— "The old Parish of Chippenham included."

„ 125—Though it is understood that the old Pillar and inscribed plate which once stood on "Chippenham Clift" are still in existence; since the text was printed, a *new* stone has been erected on the side of the Causeway and the *old* inscription engraved upon it—

"Hither extendeth Maud Heath's Gift
For where I stand is Chippenham Clift."

Erected in 1698, but given in 1474.

This stone neither stands on "Chippenham Clift," nor was it erected in 1698, but nearly 200 years after, in 1894; hence in a minor sense it may come under Pope's ban on the Monument of London—

"Where London's Column pointing to the skies,
Like a tall bully, lifts its head, and *lies*."

Page 126—By the Parish Council Act the Feoffees of Maud Heath's Charity may transfer the Causeway and its property to the Parish; or the Council may add Feoffees to the Trust equal in number to those on the present Board.

Page 143—The inscription on the mutilated Coffin-lid may be otherwise read;

CLERC E ALI SIT FEMME
FOVNDOVRS DE VNE CHAVNTERI
A CEST AUT

INDEX.

Alfred, 6
Alfritha 7
Alleine, Jos., 44
ALLINGTON, 17
Aqueduct, Stanley, 49
Arms of Chippenham, 13, 14
Artists, 212, 216
Ash Wednesday Sports, 204
Asser, 7
AUBREY, JOHN, 25, 43, 219
Avon River, 28
BAILIFFS, The, 75
Badgers, 90
Barretts of Tytherton, 187
Bath, 223, 225
Baynton, Sir E., 44, 127
BELLS, The, 160
Birds' Marsh, 35, 87
BOROUGH, The, 56
BOROUGH LANDS, 81
Bowden Hill, 45
Boville, Col., 43
BOWLES, Canon, 31, 33, 45, 50, 520
Bowood, 43, 221
Bremhill, 227
BRITTON, JOHN, 84, 93, 235
Burnet, Bp. 81

Calne, 4
CAUSEWAY, The, 95
CAUSEWAY, MAUD HEATH'S, 120
CHAP HAM, 2
CELTIC and SAXON WORDS, 195
CHANTRIES, 143
    St. John Baptist, 143
    St. Katharine, 145
    St. Mary, 143
Charity Commissioners
CHARITIES, 162
Charles II., 62
Charters, 58
CHIPPENHAM PARISH, 55
    Bailiffs, 75
    Borough, 56
    Causeway, 95
    Charters, 58
    Church, 141
    Cross, 89
    Geology, 24
    Houses, 83
    Manor, 3
    Market, 90
    Members of Parliament, 47
    Name, 2
    Pillory, 80

INDEX.   245

Plague, 98
Pump, 86
Riots, 107
School, 103
Streets, 83
Taverns, 83
Tokens, 92
Town, 82
Town Hall, 63
Churchill's Poems, 91
Church of St. Andrew, 141
CHURCHWARDENS' RECORDS, 160
CIVIL WAR, 127
Cloth, 91
Cock, Rev. Robert, 16
COCKLEBURY, 103
Coleridge, 224
Common, Langley Burrell, 41
Common, Langley Fitzurse, 41
COMMUNION PLATE, 159
Convents, 50
CORN, 90
Cornish Army, 130
Corsham, 4
Crabbe, 225
Cromwell, 140, 210
Cross, Market, 89
Danby, Earl of, 217
Danes, The, 7
Danvers, Sir J. 14, 217
D'Arcy, Lord, 64
Devizes, Siege of, 131
Domesday Book, 8
Dowett, Major, 38
Draycot Park, 42

Drogo, 48
Drought, 190
Edward the Confessor, 7
Edward I. 49, 53, 67
Edward II. 53
Edward VI. 63
Egerton, Lord Chancellor, 61
Elections, 70
Elizabeth, Queen, 67, 93
Enclosure Act, 39
ELLIOTT, ROBERT, 212
Evelyn, John, 44
Excommunication, Letters of, 156
Fairfax, Gen., 107, 140
Feoffees, Church, 154
Fish of the Avon, 29
Fitzwarine, Fulke, 51
FOGHAMSHIRE, 17
FORESTS of CHIPPENHAM, 19
Foss Way, 3
Fowlswick, 85
Fox, George, 211
Frampton, Rev. T. 99
Gaol, Borough, 81
GARDEN OF WILTS, 35
Gardiner, Thos., Mem. Book, 189
Gascelyn, Godfrey, 13
GEOLOGY OF CHIPPENHAM, 24
George III. 91
Godarville, Walter de, 13
Goldney, 68, 111
Gray's Elegy, 209, 235
Hardenhuish, 35
Harold, 8
HEATH MAUD, 120

Heber, Bishop, 43
Henry VIII. 52
Henry, Prince, 13
HERBERT, GEORGE, 217
Hermit of Chippenham, 97
HEWLETT, JAMES, 212
Hodierne the Nurse, 14
Hoare, Sir R. G., 46
Holland, Judge, 34, 85
Honour in Foxes, 36
HOSE, OUTRAGEOUS, 75
HOUSES, 83
Hubba, 6
Hundred of Chippenham, 5
Hungerford, Edward, 14, 15, 127
Hungerford, Walter Lord, 13, 59
Husee, Nicholas, 14
Ina, 10
Inlands, 21
Irish Melodies, 232
Isabella, Queen, 52
Ivy, The, 35
JACKSON, CANON, 238
Jacobs of Norton, 18
James I., 61
James II., 62
John, Prince, 51
John, King, 51
Keble, John, 44
Ken, Bishop, 226
Kent, Richard, 62
Kington St. Michael, 203, 219, 237
Lacock Abbey, 144
Langley Burrell, 35, 37, 39, 188
Langley Fitzurse, 41

Lansdown, Battle of, 129
Lansdowne, Henry, Marquis of, 231
Latimer, Bishop, 52
Linnæus, 44
LOCKSWELL, 31, 49, 86, 88
LONDON, FIRE of, 105
Long, Sir James, 127, 137, 139
LOWDON MANOR, 15
Malmesbury, 12, 128
Marden River, 30, 87
Markets, 90
Marriage under Commonwealth, 158
Mary, Queen, 56, 58, 81
Massey, Gen. 133
Maud, Empress, 16, 48, 146
MAUD HEATH'S CAUSEWAY, 20
Melksham, 12, 57
Melodies, Irish, 232
MEMBERS OF PARLIAMENT, 67
Memorandum Book of Thomas Gardiner, 189
Mills, 11
Missel Thrushes and Squirrels, 37
MONKTON, 16, 34
Monkton Farley Priory, 16, 17, 146
Monumental Inscriptions, 165
MOORE, THOMAS, 225, 228, 230
Mortimer, Roger, 52
MUGGLETON, LUDOVIC, 210
NATIVES, DISTINGUISHED, 210
Neeld, Sir John, 34
Neff, Felix, 26

INDEX.

Nethermore, 23, 49, 55
NOMINA VILLARUM, 113
Ogbourne, St. Mary, 112
Ordnances and Decrees, 76
Palace Square, 5, 84
Parish Council, 243
PARLIAMENT, MEMBERS of, 67
PAUL'S, St. CHURCH, 191
Pavely, 15
Peckingel, 25, 30
Pembroke, Earl of, 67
Penn, William, 211
Perambulation of Forests, 20, 21
PERSONS OF NOTE, 217
Pewsham, 20, 22, 56
Piedmont, 26
PILLORY, 80
PLAGUE, The, 98
Population of Chippenham, 12
Popham, Sir F., 82, 161
Provis, Alfred, 213
Provis, John, 213
Prynne, Sir Gilbert, 17, 183
Rain, Great, 191
Rebus on Chippenham, 242
REGISTERS, The, 154
Richard I., 14, 49
Richard II., 50
RIOTS, 107
Rogers, Samuel, 232
Romans, 3
Roundway Down, Battle of, 131
ROWDON, 14, 134
Sacrilege, 152
Salisbury Plain, 69

SCHOOL, The, 103
SCOTT, Dr. 209
Serfs, 9
Seymour, Sir E., 17
SHELDON, 13, 184
Sheriff in Prison, 73
SHERIFFS of WILTS, 116
Slaughterford, 146
Sloperton Cottage, 231
Small Pox, 99
Sonnets, Bowles's, 224
Southey, 225, 228, 237
Spa, Chippenham, 34
Spencer, Hugh de, 52
STANLEY ABBEY, 48
Stephen, K., 12
Stephens, Col., 134
STOCKS, The, 81
Stokes, Edward, 188
STREETS, 82
Swineherds, 11
"*Sylva*," 44
Tanner, Bishop, 239
TAVERNS, 83
Taxes, 8
TERRÆ REGIS, 48
Tithes, Rectorial, 148
TOKENS, 92
TOWN OF CHIPPENHAM, 82
TOWN HALL, 63
Town Mill, 11, 106
TOWN PUMP, 86
TOWN WELL, 87
Trade, 90
Trench, Archbishop, 52

Trowbridge, 12
Tytherton Lucas, 148, 187
Uphill, 222
VICAR OF CHIPPENHAM, 146
Vicarage House, 35
Vicar of Kington St. Michael, 203
Villan, 10
VILLA REGIA, 2, 4
Waller, Sir Wm., 128
Walton, Isaac, 218
Warminster, 4, 12
WELLS, 33

Weston super Mare, 222, 228
Wick Hill, 42
William I., 8
"*Wiltshire Rant,*" 188
"*Wiltshire, Beauties of,*" 237
Wiltshire Archæo. Mag. 240
WILTS, GARDEN of, 35
WILTS, SHERIFFS of, 116
Woodruffe, Wm., 30, 103
WORDS, CELTIC AND SAXON, 195
Wordsworth, 226
Wykeham, Bishop, 147
Wyle, Walter de, Bishop, 50